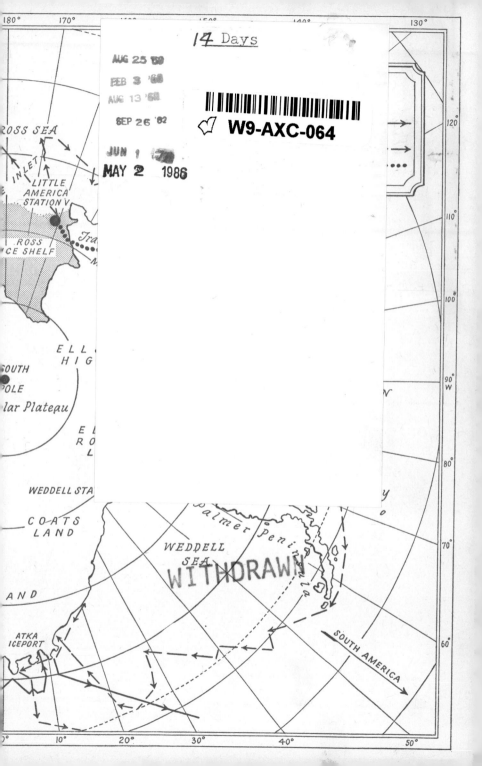

ANTARCTIC ASSAULT

ANTARCTIC ASSAULT

Commander
Paul W. Frazier, USN

ILLUSTRATED WITH PHOTOGRAPHS

DODD, MEAD & COMPANY, NEW YORK
1958

Library of Congress Catalog Card Number: 58-13094

Printed in the United States of America
by Vail-Ballou Press, Inc., Binghamton, N. Y.

To my wife, Marty

FOREWORD

COMMANDER FRAZIER has written an accurate and fascinating account of modern Antarctic exploration. From experience, as well as from a keen sense of values, he has outlined the dramatic struggles and conquests of areas of this frozen world, yet he has not forgotten those intimate and personal incidents that are woven into the bigger picture. In a real sense, this personal saga contributes substantially to the knowledge of the last great geographic frontier. He has done so with the accuracy of a historian and the drama of a novelist. His book will be welcome reading to those who want a tang of realism, first-hand, of the world's last frontier, told with restraint and frankness.

Commander Frazier displayed leadership, ability, attention to duty and courage of a very high order. He has my deep and enduring gratitude and admiration as a naval officer in Antarctic Operations, as well as my appreciation for putting into book form, experiences which will always be remembered and appreciated by his associates and by me, and shared with a wide circle of readers.

GEORGE DUFEK
Rear Admiral, USN (Ret.)

INTRODUCTION

SEVERAL events in recent years have combined to focus a lot of interest on the Antarctic continent. Men have plunged to their deaths in airplane crashes while others have fallen with their tractors into crevasses and the icy seas. Ships have been crushed in the jaws of closing ice.

On the more cheerful side of the ledger, man has landed an airplane at the geographic South Pole for the first time, several thousand square miles of unexplored territory have been seen and mapped, huge tractor trains have navigated the icecap to points several hundred miles inland, and airplanes have dropped cargo to build a camp at the South Pole.

Houses fabricated in America, Japan, England, Russia, and half a hundred other nations of the world have been ferried into the Antarctic by ship and by aircraft to be assembled on the ice.

Individually the stories reflect drama, adventure, catastrophe, heroism, and accomplishment. Taken collectively as pieces of a jig-saw puzzle, they spell out the problems that have been overcome by Americans and men of many nations who went quietly about their task of building houses on the ice for the scientists who are now taking part in the International Geophysical Year.

I have been privileged, as a staff officer under Rear Admiral George J. Dufek, to play a part in the building of seven American bases on the South Polar continent.

When the United States Navy was given the responsibility for providing support for American scientists assigned to Antarctic science studies, Admiral Dufek, the task force commander, began looking for experienced officers and men to get the job done. The call came to me as a welcome relief from the rigors of life in the Destroyer Navy. I had experienced the thrill of Antarctic, as well as Arctic, exploration several years before, and I volunteered, quite eager to match wits with the ice again.

PAUL W. FRAZIER

CONTENTS

ILLUSTRATIONS

(All illustrations are official U. S. Navy photographs.)

[xiii]

ILLUSTRATIONS

OPERATION WINDMILL

I ────────────────────────

I FIRST saw the South Polar continent in the fall of 1947 when, as a Lieutenant Commander, I was assigned as operations officer to the commander task force 39 on the icebreaker *Burton Island* for Antarctic Operation Windmill. The code name for our expedition was derived from the fact that we would put helicopters to extensive use in the Antarctic for the first time.

Our task force of two ships was puny when compared to the 4,000-man complement which had comprised Operation Highjump a year earlier. Airmen of that force had sighted and mapped a greater amount of Antarctica's face in one summer's operation than man had explored in all previous expeditions combined.

But there was one big hitch. Unless the map makers in Washington could be sure of the exact geographical location of certain mountains, capes, and other landmarks that could be used to "tie in" with the aerial photographs, the entire mapping mission would have been in vain.

Precise navigational aids were pitifully inadequate because the little amount of charting that had been done in the Antarctic had been accomplished with crude instruments by sealers and whalers who had intentionally obscured information to avoid revealing choice hunting grounds.

We put out from the United States in the icebreakers *Burton Island* and *Edisto* in the fall of 1947 to take maximum advantage of the Antarctic summer and its twenty-four-hour days of sunlight in establishing ground control points that could be used to identify the aerial photographs which had been made the previous year.

During the trip south I developed a lifelong feeling for icebreakers as a class of ship. My teacher was Frank Dawley, executive officer of the *Burton Island*. Frank and I would tour the vessel together, and he seemed to enjoy pointing out the advantages of icebreakers over "ordinary" warships.

"Here is every ship the Navy has—rolled into one," he would brag.

"She has the roll of a destroyer, the armor plate of a battleship, the flight deck of an aircraft carrier, the range of a tanker, but, best of all, the comforts of home."

Frank reminded me of a mature Jack Armstrong. He could do anything: operate ham radio equipment, repair watches, or run a lathe. He had the only pictures I have ever seen of a killer whale devouring seals in the Bay of Whales.

Frank was a stickler for discipline and cleanliness. Consequently the *Burton Island* was the cleanest ship afloat.

The *Burton Island* is considered a "Wind Class" icebreaker because the first ships of her type were named *Eastwind, Westwind,* and *Southwind.* The Wind Class breakers displace six thousand tons and have accommodations for about three hundred men.

They are run by six Diesel engines that generate ten thousand shaft horsepower, sufficient to furnish power to a large city. This energy provides the force that permits them to smash through ice fifteen feet thick, and the great weight allows them to ride up on, then crush down through

[4]

ice that is too heavy to be broken by frontal attack.

In appearance, icebreakers are the most ungainly ships afloat. On the horizon they resemble battleships. From astern they look like aircraft carriers even though their flight deck is large enough for only two helicopters.

Their round bottom resembles a long watermelon because there is no keel. Rounded lines permit the ship to ride up on the hard sea ice, and sheer weight does the rest.

Helicopters operate from the icebreakers to scout the ice pack for cracks or leads, and they also ferry men and equipment ashore. Each ship has a crow's-nest, heated of course, high up on its mast where a lookout can scan the route ahead when it is too rough to launch helicopters.

Engine controls are located in the pilot house, on each wing of the bridge, and at the stern on the flight deck. This gives the conning officer a complete view of the sides of the ship and helps him to keep the propellers away from large pieces of ice.

The propellers are giants of special steel alloy that can bite through hunks of ice the size of a house; but they are vulnerable when struck by "blue ice," whose saline content has drained downward into the sea and left the ice as hard as steel.

By filling the heeling and trim tanks with fuel, the icebreaker's range is increased to such an extent that it can go around the world three times without refueling. This quantity of fuel is most important in polar latitudes because of the distance to the nearest refueling point. Then, too, an icebreaker sometimes spends a full day bucking a few hundred yards of ice.

We left from San Pedro aboard the *Burton Island,*

and the *Edisto* sailed from Boston. The ships met off Panama and followed tracks five miles apart to chart the sea bottom with our depth-measuring instruments on the voyage south. The cruise was pleasant, and we got to know our companions as well as our ship.

To Frank Dawley the most important word, and certainly the most commendable trait of icebreaker people, was *patience*. He stressed this as we steamed south.

"If you are banging your head against the ice and can't make any headway, stop and wait. You might wait for a few hours or a few days; but eventually the wind will shift and the pack will loosen, and you can proceed.

"When things are going real bad there is only one way they can change, and that is for the better."

His advice proved sound on many occasions.

We stopped for a final liberty in Samoa, and Commander Gerald Ketchum, the task force commander, outlined his plans.

"We will proceed to Scott Island, look at the ice pack, and head west, skirting the pack to chart its edge during this time of year.

"When we arrive at the western edge of the Shackleton Ice Shelf we will head south for Haswell Island in the vicinity of Mount Gauss. We have six ground control points to set up in this area, and I will divide them between the two ships.

"After we have secured these stations we will head east to Vincennes Bay and to other ground control points in the Bunger Oasis area."

The phrase "Bunger Oasis" caught my attention. I, like several million Americans, had read press accounts reporting the discovery of a veritable oasis in the ice-locked continent during Operation Highjump. A Navy pilot named Bunger was reported to have landed his seaplane in the fresh water of a mountain lake. The water wasn't only fresh; it was warm, the stories implied. The crew of each icebreaker hoped their ship would be chosen to revisit this mythical-sounding paradise. They felt confident they would find lush vegetation; they hoped to find grass-skirted native girls in the barren continent that had supported no human life for ninety million years.

"From there," Ketchum continued, "we establish other control points on our way to Little America. At Little America we will dig out various items of equipment left behind last year and test them.

"Time permitting, we will establish other control points eastward to Marguerite Bay on the Palmer Peninsula where we will visit Finn Ronne and see if he needs any assistance in gretting free of the bay ice."

Commander Finn Ronne had sailed as head of a private expedition to the Palmer Peninsula during the period that Operation Highjump was being conducted. He had intentionally allowed his ship, the *Port of Beaumont*, to be frozen in when the summer ended, and had lived ashore with his crew in a camp that had been erected on the ice.

Ketchum explained that all aircraft would carry two weeks' supply of survival rations, sleeping bags, and first-aid kits. The crash of a seaplane during Highjump was still a timely subject with us because the crew had remained stranded on the ice for two weeks before rescue came.

"All boats will be equipped with radios and rations," he said. "We won't take any more chances than we have to.

"When in the ice we will usually break in column so

that the icebreaker astern can save fuel.

"Any questions?"

Commander Pete Folger, skipper of the *Edisto*, answered: "Yes, sir. When is the steward going to fill our coffee cups?"

2

"GET up, Paul," my roommate said. "You have the first under-way watch."

Our room was hot even during the early morning. The sun beat down on the decks, and most of the heat had been trapped in the ship. An icebreaker is designed for cold weather, and its bulkheads are insulated with about six inches of cork to keep the heat inside. They are miserable ships in the tropics.

"Make the signal to get under way, and proceed out of port," Commander Ketchum directed.

The signalmen were grouchy, with reason. They had exercised an age-old Navy tradition the previous night by allowing all senior men to go ashore on liberty while they left an apprentice with the watch. He forgot to cover the flag bags during an early morning rain squall, and the flags were drenched. When the signal was made, the flags hung limp on their halyards.

From the *Edisto* four identical wet flags were two-blocked. Their signal gang had observed the same trick liberty arrangements.

As soon as we were at sea I had the signalmen make the signal to air bunting. The task force steamed south-ward with every flag in the flag bags flying. Navy regulations don't cover the contingencies likely to be encountered as a result of frozen signal flags and, being a conscientious young watch officer, I wasn't taking any chances.

The further south we sailed, the rougher the sea became. Weather changed from bad, to worse, to horrible. We slowed to four knots to keep steerageway, and our round-bottom ships rolled unmercifully. We wallowed in the troughs of the mountainous seas which frequently struck us full on the beam.

Cups and saucers rattled across the wardroom tables and smashed on deck. Fuel in the tank below the wardroom gurgled and sloshed. There were baffles to slow down the movement of the fuel, but they didn't have much effect.

Rough as it was, Frank Dawley still insisted on soup as the first course. A Navy soup bowl is a shallow, wide container. Every member of the mess sat with his bowl in his left hand, tilting it in rhythm to the ship's roll and trying to scoop a spoonful when balance seemed possible. Chairs were lashed to the deck so they would not slide.

I growled to Frank that it would take a five-armed gentleman to get by in his wardroom. He would have to have a left hand to hold his bowl, a right hand for the spoon, a third hand to pass the plate of crackers, a fourth to keep his plate from jumping around, and a fifth to hold his chair during the most severe rolls.

But Frank was exec, and we had our soup. It was particularly good in the middle of the morning if you could sneak past the executive officer and drink it from a cup while standing. The big soup kettle stayed hot constantly.

Fog settled on us, and we commenced sounding signals in accord with the International Rules of the Road. There wasn't another ship, except the *Edisto*, within a thousand miles. But the book says to sound fog signals, so every two minutes there was a long blast on the whistle.

At least once a day the whistle stuck and the note would extend for several minutes, until an engineer could cut the source of air, repair the trouble, and return the monotonous blasts to schedule.

In two days the fog changed to snow. There is a repulsive sort of beauty to be seen when you are riding out a heavy sea in a snowstorm. The flakes, blown furiously by the wind, seemed to make a halo over the dingy-blue valleys and mountains of waves, which at times were higher than our mast. When we rode to the crest of a big one the valley seemed several hundred feet below us.

We wallowed through the "roaring forties," the "furious fifties," and the "screaming sixties" of south latitude. Gale after gale buffeted our sturdy ships as we plunged and rolled nearer and nearer the ice pack which would give us relief from the miserable rolling and pounding of the sea.

The public address system blasted away: "Iceberg bearing one seven five degrees true, distance twenty miles." The berg had been picked up by radar and was not yet visible to the eye.

The radar operator watched each sweep of his scope and plotted the movement of the berg. "The iceberg will pass to port bearing zero nine zero degrees true, distance two miles," said the squawk box.

Word of the first berg brought all camera fans topside. Men who had been green with seasickness for days mustered enough courage to join the rest of the ship's company and click their shutters. It was the first iceberg for most of us, and we weren't going to miss it.

I honestly believe there was more film exposed on that scrawny little berg than on anything else the rest of the trip. Several times on that first trip to Antarctica, and on subsequent trips, I heard conjecture that the Eastman Kodak Company was responsible for persuading the American government to send expeditions to the Antarctic. The company's stock must surely rise from the quantity of film sold to the sailors.

A betting pool had been formed, and a hassel now developed as to whether the official time of sighting the berg was that in the radar log or the time it was sighted visually by the lookout. What price modern conveniences, I mused. Frank Dawley settled the argument by splitting the pool between the holders of tickets with the visual and radar sighting times.

The berg really wasn't very much. It was weather-beaten, and sea action had washed caves in its lower sides. It was white, but a dirty white running to a deep green at the water line. It had been floating for a long time.

Next day we reached the ice pack. As far as the eye could behold, the ice cast a nearly unbroken white blanket over the seas. I had already seen oil intentionally spilled upon the water in an effort to create a sea state level enough to land a ship-based seaplane, but I had never beheld such a complete blanket applied to water as we now saw. From the icebreaker's bridge we could look some eleven miles to the horizon. There was not a break in the whiteness as far as we could see.

Toward the seaward edge of the pack we noticed penguins playing, and once more the cameras began clicking. The birds seemed as interested in us as we were in them.

I had assumed that the ice would extend above the water, but it did not. Regardless of its thickness, I learned that sea ice remains level with the surface.

Long sea swells from storms to the north caused the pack to heave up and down at its outer perimeter. The

Burton Island nosed into the ice and the ship bobbed, breaking her way toward Scott Island. In the pack we were finally on an even keel as we punched our way. To me, a beginner, the ice seemed heavy; but it didn't even slow the ship down.

Scott Island showed up as a small "pip" on our radar, and we turned west, now that our navigation was verified. The lookouts strained for a glimpse of the famous landmark, and the navigator was very anxious to hear their first sighting report.

Finally the bare-faced, barren rock came into view. It is amazing how closely Scott Island resembles the Rock of Gibraltar from a distance. Studying the rock through binoculars, I realized instantly why it had been declared impossible to erect a weather station there during Operation Highjump. The great stone face of the island, beaten smooth by countless blizzards, allowed no access to the top from its sheer, steep sides. The sailing directions said Scott Island was a quarter-mile long and a half-mile wide; that it had been seen first in 1902 by Captain Robert Falcon Scott.

I expressed my relief to Fred Robinson, my roommate, when my navigation had been checked. He in turn told me the foolproof way to navigate in the Antarctic. His method, he said, was called "Martini Navigation":

"After a few days without sun sights, when you don't know where the hell you're at, stop everything. Get a bottle of gin and a bottle of vermouth. Take a glass, and reach over the side and scoop up some ice. Be sure you take it off the top of the pack, otherwise it will be salty.

"Put five parts of gin and one part vermouth on top of the ice, and stir gently. Don't bruise the gin.

"Pour the mixture into a Martini glass, and sit down. Begin drinking it. Invariably, guests will drop by, so pour them a glass too.

"The discussion will get around to how you made the Martini, and someone will comment that he usually builds them seven to one, eight to one, or, if he's gutless, maybe just two to one.

"He will imply that you don't know how to mix a Martini.

"If he knows so damn much, you ask the SOB *where he is* and get your navigational fix from him!"

After several days of fog, rain, and snow I began to wish I had some gin and vermouth to test Fred's method. There was plenty of ice.

We took a westerly course from Scott Island, and on December 18 emerged from the pack. Keeping it in sight we headed west toward Shackleton Ice Shelf and our first six ground control points.

The *Hashidate Maru*, a Japanese whaler with twenty-three catcher boats, sent us weather reports every four hours. But because of the inherent secrecy of good whaling ships, she wouldn't give us her position. Her weather reports were accurate, but they were no good to us because we couldn't plot them on our chart.

We also contacted the *Balaena*, a British whaler, and exchanged weather information, but she wouldn't reveal her position either.

On Christmas Eve we sighted a whaling ship we identified as the *Southern Harvest*, also British. We exchanged Christmas greetings and weather reports, but because we were in the same vicinity her reports were useless.

She no doubt moved elsewhere as soon as we radioed our position.

Christmas Day we headed south and encountered heavy ice west of Shackleton. The *Edisto* was in the lead, breaking, while the *Burton Island* tagged along behind.

Now I began to watch an icebreaker in her element. The *Edisto* had all her six engines on the line. She would charge the ice, ride up on it, crack through and still make only a dent. She would back free, charge pellmell again, and achieve the same results. "When do we start practicing patience?" I wondered. A fog rolled in, and we hove to.

In such a sea of ice, rather a *field* of ice, light can do funny things. In a dead fog, so thick that we couldn't see the forecastle from the bridge, photographers recorded the highest light-meter readings they had ever seen.

Frank explained that we were not in a fog; we were in a "white-out." He also explained the light-meter phenomenon. "It's refraction," he said. "The white ice below bounces light rays up against the white cloud overcast, then it reflects to the white sea ice and back again. It intensifies itself during the series of bounces, even though the sun is completely obscured."

By now there was no darkness. When somebody said "night" he meant that period between eight P.M. and eight A.M., even though the next sunset would occur in March. We enjoyed our Christmas dinner while waiting for the weather to clear.

About eleven P.M. the white-out lifted. We could see no open leads, so Ketchum called in Dick Long, the senior pilot, and told me to accompany him on the first helicopter reconnaissance.

We flew to the southward looking for leads. I charted conditions while Dick flew. We weren't airborne more than five minutes when I noticed we were heading back to the ship.

"What's up, Dick?" I asked over the microphone. "I have a couple of leads plotted, plus an open pool, but we haven't gone far enough yet to justify our flight."

"See that western horizon? That fog or haze is going to be on us in a few minutes, and I don't have good radio communications with the ship," he told me. "Know what it's like to fly in a white-out? You lose equilibrium and you can't tell if you're flying on your backside or your stomach. We're getting back while we can."

In the few minutes it took us to reach the ship and hover over the flight deck the white-out was on us again. Dick didn't wait for all the landing preparations. He set the small helicopter down hard on the flight deck and grinned. The white-out was so complete I could barely see my way forward to the bridge to report the meager results of our reconnaissance.

Commander Ketchum and I bent over the chart as I sketched where the open water pool had been sighted. "The pool is about seven miles, bearing one eight zero. The lead is about ten miles south of the pool and runs southeast."

"Glad to see you made it back before this white-out set in, Paul," he said.

He was glad!

Commander Ketchum worked up a grin, and I knew that he was fully aware of my near-miss during the reconnaissance. Already I felt an affinity toward the Commander. In years to come we would sail together many times, and he would become the most trusted and dependable of

During an enthusiastic farewell to the task force given by the people of New Zealand, a sailor falls into the water from one of the ships.

The largest column of ships ever to transit the ice pack heads for the Antarctic through the Ross Sea led by the icebreaker USS Glacier.

RADM R. E. Byrd, RADM G. Dufek, CDR E. H. Mahes, Capt. C. A. Thomas and the author meet for a conference aboard the USS *Glacier*.

Adelie penguins on Ross Island

Dufek's Volunteers. But his smiling concern over that chart table was really the start of my deep friendship with him. His expression gave me new confidence because here was a man who didn't get excited about anything—even losing *me*, I thought later.

We sat there for three hours while the white-out alternately lifted and settled. It was like being inside a full bottle of milk. There was no horizon, no ground, no sky; only white.

Finally the weather cleared, and another flight confirmed open water twelve miles south. I was awakened by the jarring feeling of the ship breaking ice.

Two days later we picked up Drygalski Island on radar. The *Burton Island* and *Edisto* parted company, and each proceeded in open water to its assigned ground control point area.

We passed Drygalski close aboard. It was a high, ice-capped mountain, about nine miles in diameter, in the middle of nowhere. The book said it was 1,200 feet high, but it looked higher. We were about forty-five miles off the Queen Mary Coast, which had been sighted first by Sir Douglas Mawson in 1912.

Burton Island's first ground control point was number four, Haswell Island. Preparations were made to launch a helicopter reconnaissance flight, but the weather again turned bad. Fifty-knot winds screamed through the helicopter's lashings. Flying in such weather would be impossible, so we hove to and waited for the storm to abate. The *Edisto* was hove to, forty miles to the west. Patience, the man had said.

About midnight the weather cleared, and pilots were called from their warm bunks to make the flight. We estimated Haswell Island to be about 139 degrees true, thirty-one miles distant. We flew out on that bearing and located our destination.

The ship broke ice to within fifteen miles of Haswell Island by morning, then moored to the fast ice and sent a landing party ashore by tracked vehicles, called weasels. No sooner had the party established a tent camp than weather closed in. No navigational sun shots were possible for the remainder of the day.

By foot we scouted our surroundings. Haswell Island was roughly rectangular, about half a mile long and three-quarters of a mile wide. It had three ridges running parallel with a small lake between the second and third ridge. Dr. Apfel, the geologist, estimated the lake to be about twenty feet deep.

As visibility improved, we could see other islands to the south and west. Small Adélie penguins from the rookery on the island squawked their hellos and waddled bravely up to us as if to shake hands. That occasion was ten years ago, and to this day I stop dead in my tracks to watch the antics of the penguins. They will never cease to amaze me by their curiosity, their brazenness that no doubt is nurtured on the fact that they have never had to defend themselves from land enemies. They have never learned to fear.

The surveyor set up an astronomical station on a prominent pile of rocks to begin taking his sun lines, but again the sun disappeared. He finally got his first sight on the third day, and by noon had finished enough sequence shots so that there was no doubt of the accuracy of his fix.

The precise fixing of a position by sun lines alone is very difficult. The surveyor works on the premise that his timepiece is exactly correct. With a sextant or theodolite, he "pulls" the sun down to the horizon line by a principle of optics. That way he verifies the exact altitude of the sun from a known angle. He takes periodic shots of the sun from other angles as it rises to its zenith at noon and declines. Then, on the point at which the lines cross in a hairline area, the position where he is standing to make his observations is accurately fixed. If another land mass bears so many degrees and is so many miles from that known point, its exact location is known also. We were finally doing what we had come eleven thousand miles to accomplish.

We recalled the weasels to pick us up and return us to the *Burton Island*. One broke down on the way back, causing a delay, but at last we steamed in open water off the edge of the fast ice and the captain turned the *Burton Island* up to fourteen knots to regain his schedule. Waves from our turbulent wake splashed against the ice a few hundred yards to starboard. It was obvious that if we spent five days at each of the control stations we would never complete all of the stations assigned. Speed was paramount!

The "pings" of the fathometer, our depth-measuring device, were audible on the bridge. There was a low-pitched outgoing ping, then a higher-pitched return signal. For a while the response was steady. Then suddenly the instrument indicated that the water was getting shallow alarmingly fast.

"All engines back full!" the captain shouted.

The *Burton Island* seemed to squat, stop, tremble, then, as the engines reversed, to sit there panting.

We on the bridge were panting too. It had been so long since we had broken ice that we were charging pell-mell at the nearest ice in sight when the fathometer tipped us off that we were reaching shoal water. *What we had taken for a piece of floating ice was actually the peak of a nearly submerged island!* Two more ship lengths and we would have tested *Burton Island*'s bow against solid rock.

We named the uncharted islet Burton Island Rock and made it ground control point number seven.

Skirting the shoal area, we hove to near the towering cliffs of the Shackleton Ice Shelf. The shelf stuck out from the Queen Mary Coast more than a hundred miles. Its width stretched between five degrees of longitude, and it towered a hundred fifty feet into the air. Its bottom lay somewhere below the water—about fifty fathoms deep, we guessed.

The view of an Antarctic ice shelf from seaward is hard to describe. Along the top it extends as level as the palm of one's hand for many miles. Its perpendicular edge is a sheer ninety-degree drop into the sea. Tidal action tends to undermine the lower section and often creates a "tunnel" large enough to enter with a lifeboat. In a storm, the whole seaward edge of the ice shelf surges gently up and down with the action of the water. Eventually, this motion causes a great chunk to break off from the mother shelf, and an iceberg is born. So large is the berg on occasion that, moving with the currents and the winds, it eventually becomes a menace to navigation several thousand miles from its birthplace.

Lieutenant Charles Wilkes, an American, had first sighted this shelf in 1840, but it went nameless until Douglas Mawson, an Australian explorer, christened it after the Antarctic explorer Sir Ernest Shackleton in 1911.

A high-latitude radio black-out now cut us off from communication with the *Edisto* to the west. Only after three days of silence did the black-out lift, and then *Edisto* informed us that their landing party ashore hadn't been heard from for two days.

The report alarmed me. Suppose a blizzard or a prolonged white-out had moved in on the men. They could have panicked and stumbled blindly toward what they thought was the point where they would be picked up, only to walk off the ice to their death in the sea.

Immediately we dispatched helicopters, which located them only a few miles away from their ship where they had stopped to try to raise the *Edisto* by radio.

By this time, we were behind on our assignment, and we were making a hurried attempt to return to schedule. We decided to establish point number six by helicopter lift instead of sending men across the ice in weasels.

On its first pass, the helicopter made a crash landing in the vicinity of the protruding rocks. I marveled at the patience Commander Ketchum could display in the face of repeated frustrations. Only the helicopter's pontoons were damaged; but the survey party was far from its destination, and it would take more precious time to get the men to the place where they were needed. We had to divert another helicopter to evacuate the men and to carry tools to repair the damaged aircraft.

Edisto was ordered to join us at best speed. Weather might close in at any time and prevent evacuation for days. *Edisto* arrived the next day, and her helicopter took out a repair crew and tools to bend the pontoons back into shape and permit our helicopter to take off. The damaged aircraft flew safely back to the *Burton Island*.

During the twenty-four-hour period the party was stranded, weather had been good. The surveyor and his chief quartermaster stepped out of the nosed-over plane and began shooting sun sights. They completed their station in the short period they waited for rescue.

Edisto was sent back to complete point three. She would rejoin *Burton Island* when her station was finished, and then both ships would break their way northward.

The hydrographers worked as quickly as they could. There are some things which can be forced, but the orbit of the sun is not one of them. Shots taken at less than fifteen-minute intervals are nearly worthless because the angle of the sun changes too little from the preceding shot. So the navigators shot their sights and prayed that the sun would not be obscured until the sequence was completed.

Ashore, the hydrographers could concern themselves merely with the availability of a sun to shoot, while on the ships we were concerned not only with their shots, but getting them back alive so that we could race for the next assignment.

Work in the area was completed January 5th, and both ships began breaking ice toward the destination we were all anxious to see—Bunger Oasis.

3 ——————————

BOTH icebreakers paralleled the western edge of the
Shackleton Ice Shelf as we headed northward. We slugged
away at the sea ice for four hours and advanced only four
miles. Ahead, the ice looked even more formidable.

We reversed course and began backtracking to open
water. We were almost in the clear when the *Edisto* hit
rough ice on the windward side of a large tabular iceberg.
By radar the berg measured three miles long.

Edisto charged the ice with all her power, trying to
force her snub bow through the narrow strip of tough pack
ice that separated her from open water. Each time she
charged, she seemed merely to dent the steel-hard ice.

Seeing her problem, the *Burton Island*'s skipper forced
his ship past the other side of the iceberg and broke through
into open water. He spun the ship around and headed back
to help cut the *Edisto* out.

When we came close aboard *Edisto* we could see that
she was being held fast in the ice. Her giant "heeling" tanks
were being employed. This is a method of shifting liquid
from one side of the ship to the other to create an artificial
roll. The roll, in turn, causes the ship to "seat" herself
deeper and deeper in the ice until she creates a rupture and
is free. The principle is a great deal like a broad-beamed
gentleman jockeying and shifting his hips to fit himself into
a crowded subway seat just vacated by a child.

Before heeling tanks were invented, a ship's entire
crew was paraded on deck in one compact group. They

would race together from one side of the ship to the other to create the same kind of roll. That process was known in the days of sailing vessels as "sallying ship."

Aboard the *Burton Island* we secretly hoped we would have to "rescue" the *Edisto* from her plight. Such a feat would be told and retold in bars from Montevideo to Boston and from Christchurch to San Pedro, wherever icebreaker men met, if only we could save them before they saved themselves.

The *Burton Island* hit the ice wall at fourteen knots. Our six thousand tons barely made a dent in the ice as we came to a sudden, shuddering stop.

Now both ships backed their engines at full power. We could see that *Edisto* was no longer held fast. We lay to and watched her charge the pack once more at full power. By now it was a race to see which ship broke through first. If *Edisto* broke through, the barroom jokes would be at our expense.

Edisto hurled her weight at the ice once more, only to ride up over the edge and slide down again. The dent her bow made was hardly ten feet.

Now *Edisto* lay to, and we charged from our side. We made ten feet. *Edisto* charged again for ten feet, and *Burton Island* made another ten feet. It was like the brand of "power" football played by Big Ten schools in the thirties.

Burton Island withdrew and gained full power as she bristled toward the ice once more, cocky as a bantam rooster charging a bulldog. We felt the bow rise into the air, and a shudder ran the length of the ship. Our momentum was enough to carry us through the pack. We could brag that we had cut the *Edisto* out, but the look of concern on the captain's face caused us to wonder if our victory had been an empty one. He thought a propeller had been damaged during the crucial moment the ship had shuddered so badly. Inspection by divers revealed that we had suffered no damage, however.

With the *Edisto* free, we steamed westward in open water. Actually we were in an open pool, surrounded by the pack. We looked for a lead, or crack, that we could follow without such difficulty as both ships had just experienced.

Commander Ketchum ordered a long-range airplane reconnaissance flight when helicopter reconnaissance failed to discover a lead. Our amphibian plane was lowered into the water. The taxi-way it would use for take-off was carefully patrolled by men in a motor launch to be sure the plane would not strike a floating piece of ice and rupture its hull during take-off.

It took some time for the pilot to warm his engines and the boat crews to clear the taxi area of ice, but finally the plane took off and disappeared from view. We tracked the craft constantly by radar. The pilot had been instructed to report every fifteen minutes.

On his first report, the pilot said: "I'm over open water. There is close, heavy pack between here and where you are. I'm returning to the ship."

Our radar indicated he was thirty miles away, bearing due north. The plane landed alongside and was hoisted aboard the *Edisto*. We got under way and headed for the open water.

Our progress was painfully slow. Alternately dumping and flooding port and starboard tanks, the ships rolled and heeled their way into heavier and heavier ice. We measured our advance in feet.

Leads appeared when the wind shifted, and two hours later our task force was in open water. By rushing things we had only succeeded in wasting fuel. Had we waited a few hours we could have penetrated the pack with four engines instead of six. On the other hand, if the wind had not shifted, we could still be waiting.

To approach Bunger Oasis the plan called for *Burton Island* to nose into the pack east of Shackleton while *Edisto* steamed twenty miles further before cutting in.

We made our rendezvous January 10, and together the ships bounced through the ice into an open-water lake surrounded by a mountainous range of tabular icebergs. The ice south of this lake was impassable.

We hove to in the open water, hoping conditions would change when the wind shifted.

Moved by unknown currents, the giant bergs began to bear down on us. We made our exit with no time to spare. The cold white jaws of two large tabular bergs closed in collision and sealed the lake astern of the *Burton Island* as she daintily picked her way out of the maze of towering white.

Icebreakers are tough, rugged, cocky ships, but I have yet to meet an icebreaker skipper who would willingly challenge an iceberg to battle. The legend is that it's what you *don't* see of an iceberg that can hurt you. The section of berg below the surface can form a slanting shoal which will capsize a ship before it strikes the visible bulk of ice.

The weather was bad for two full days. We were forced to sit and wait until we could launch a plane to get facts before we could decide on our next course.

When the weather cleared we saw an open-water lake immediately in front of us. Shifting winds had opened a channel while we lay hove to.

Edisto's airplane was launched to scout Bunger Oasis some eighty miles to the southwest while helicopters searched for leads in three directions beyond the edge of the lake we were in.

The aircraft reported another open-water lake, and the ship headed for it. Twenty hours later she was forty-five miles from Bunger Oasis. *Edisto* reported:

"Have land in sight and eighty fathoms underneath. More information within hour."

Fuel was becoming a prize item after days of running six engines against the heavy ice. Rather than waste this precious commodity to reach *Edisto*, *Burton Island* hove to and waited.

Bunger Hills, as the place is called now, was a group of moderately low-lying, rounded hills, overlain by morainic drift and notably free of ice in the summer. The hills were marked with many melt-water ponds and were bisected by a winding inlet.

At last a ship of our force had found the newspapermen's "Oasis," which by conjecture was a land free of snow because of heat rising from the bowels of the earth. On the *Burton Island* we were secretly disappointed about *Edisto* beating us there, earning the right to verify or dispel the myth.

From her advantageous position, our companion vessel staged the beach parties to investigate Bunger Oasis. We sent *Burton Island*'s helicopters to join the *Edisto* and help lift her men and equipment into the area. Weather was good and we took advantage of it. By eight P.M. the *Edisto* had a small group of men ashore, and by midnight the entire beach party had been landed.

While navigators obtained their geographic fix, Dr. E. T. Apfel, the geologist, ranged the hills collecting rock samples.

We established a relay camp on the ice about midway between the *Edisto* and the hills which would serve as a weather reporting station, a refueling camp for the helicopters, and a haven for passengers if the helicopters were forced to land during a sudden white-out.

The base equipment was delivered by Marine Captain Buck Boyd's weasels, and gasoline was flown in by helicopter. On a logistics flight the helicopter encountered a white-out near the camp and crashed. Lieutenant Jack Glenzer, the pilot, was shaken up but was not seriously injured. His plane was destroyed and is probably still sitting there on its nose with a bare rotor hub where the blades sheared off, leaving only stubs.

Weather reports looked bad January 14, so we made immediate plans to evacuate the beach party. They had no sooner reached the *Edisto* than a raging blizzard struck. Weasels evacuating men from the halfway camp were trapped in the storm some ten miles from the ship.

Buck Boyd, leader of the weasel party, showed his mettle. He got out of his machine and walked the remaining distance back to the ship ahead of the others to direct the drivers through danger areas. Some men have an instinctive sense of direction, and Buck Boyd is one of them. In the ten miles to the ship, there were many cracks in the ice, each large enough to swallow a weasel and all its occupants. Buck directed the drivers around these cracks and led them safely back. He looked like a walking snow man as he dragged himself over the side of the ship.

Aboard the *Edisto*, Dr. Apfel was too elated to concern himself with the dramatic plight of the weasel crews. He studied his rock samples carefully, comparing them with the notes he had made during his exploration of Bunger Oasis. His deductions shot holes in the newspaper reports of the previous year.

"It is an area of metamorphosed sedimentary rock," he wrote, "which has been intruded by granite and later by basalt dikes. Subsequently, a great amount of erosion exposed the formerly deeply buried rocks. Intense glacial action carved the area into a sharply irregular terrain."

Melting ice from the glacier had left a large amount of glacial material, he found, and those deposits covered practically all surfaces except such as stood at high angles.

Sediments in the thickest rocks were principally shales and sandstones. No limestones were found in place, and only a few limestone fragments were found in the glacial drift.

Sandstone beds, he told us, had been metamorphosed to quartzite which ranged from white to blue in color. It also contained garnets, especially in the vicinity of the intruded granite.

Why, we wondered, had not the reporters ballyhooed these "jewel deposits"?

While the Bunger Lakes we found had obviously been influenced by the action of a glacier, Dr. Apfel said the general region had felt the impact of a much earlier glacier. As evidence, he cited the uniform heights of the hills and ridges between the lakes.

"Bunger Lakes remain ice-free because of the relatively

low snowfall, the high heat absorption of the rock, the deflecting effect of the rock and moraine barrier along the south side, and the free drainage into the ocean," he told us.

"Further, the numerous lakes in the kettle holes are nearly all *salt-water*. Many of them contain so much dissolved salt that they are bitter to the taste."

The surface soil, he found, was marked by a white efflorescence which occurred around the margins of the water bodies and on slopes some distance from them.

"Plant and animal life were almost completely absent in the Bunger area we visited. The saline lakes have an algae growth which covers the rocks. It is brown and in some places is an eighth of an inch thick. A small network of fresh-water streams flowing from a snowbank into a saline pond had some fresh-water algae growing in them. A small moss grows on the underside of translucent pebbles and was found nowhere else."

These findings were one of the major things we had come for.

With this mission accomplished, *Burton Island* headed for point eleven. *Edisto* would follow as soon as the blizzard blew itself out.

That excursion to Bunger Oasis was a valuable object lesson to me. The tenets I learned were:

Take nothing for granted. People might exaggerate facts from sheer boredom. Others might color facts to be spectacular.

The Antarctic continent can be very deceptive. What appears innocent from aerial observation can become deadly from the surface, and vice versa.

The lesson of taking nothing for granted would prove most valuable ten years later when I found myself in command of ice parties during Operation Deep Freeze in which the nations of the world would stage the largest concentrated assault of all time against the Antarctic.

4

WHEN we had finished exploring Bunger Hills our fuel supply had become critical. In addition, the season was so late that the possibility of further exploration before we were beset by unbreakable ice had become increasingly remote. We believed that the navigational observations we had made were good enough to permit us to settle for only a few more fixes. The senior hydrographer concurred.

In company once more, the icebreakers steamed in open water toward a group of unnamed islands, any one of which would be a satisfactory control point.

Whenever numerous islands protrude sharply from the sea you expect shoaling water. Captain McDonald eased the *Burton Island* around the smaller islands, keeping one ear cocked for the pings of the fathometer which would indicate shallow water. Depth at the moment was a safe hundred fathoms, but we had indications that the bottom was shoaling.

About eight hundred yards from a large island we dropped anchor in forty-five fathoms of water. The beach looked so close we felt we could jump ashore.

This was exploration at its best; discovery in its purest form. Here were enough islands to name after every man aboard ship and still have some left over.

It was my turn to help Dr. Apfel carry his geology equipment: empty sacks and a hammer. The task appeared a snap but I had a lot to learn.

Dr. Apfel was a large man. His bulk, coupled with

what I considered at the time his advanced age, led me to believe I would have no trouble keeping pace with him.

Our boat nosed up to a rock face, and I scrambled ashore. Dr. Apfel threw his gear to me and, like a cat, jumped the small distance between the boat and the rock upon which I stood.

We strode away to chip samples of rocks and explore the area. Within an hour we had one sack filled and left it in the path we would follow back to the landing place.

We averaged a full sack an hour and put each one along the return trail. By the end of the working day all the bags were filled. The problem now was to get them back to the boat.

The island had looked big from the ship but not nearly as large as it appeared from where we stood on the opposite side from the ship when we heard the whistle, a prearranged signal that our boat would arrive shortly.

Other beach parties that had been put ashore from the ship now headed back to the boat landing. As they returned, slipping and stumbling over the icy rocks, each man grabbed a sack and returned it to the boat. Thank God, I thought.

From where we were, the most distant point, it was two miles or more to the boat. Already the full bag I carried seemed to weigh a ton. The rough edges of the rocks punched holes in my back, and the sack chafed my shoulder. Being the younger, I presumed that the "old" Doctor would soon tire and I, too, could get a rest.

The Doctor began to outdistance me.

"Hey, Doc," I shouted, "hold up and let's rest!"

By the time I overtook him he was rested and ready to start again. Every few minutes I would repeat my request and would arrive tired and winded only to find him ready to go again.

When we finally got back to the ship I was exhausted. Long after I was asleep Dr. Apfel studied his samples and made notes.

The next day it was my turn to help Dick Holl, the hydrographer. I was grateful that his only equipment was a theodolite (navigational instrument), a tripod, and a watch.

Ashore, we resembled two country boys on their way to the old fishing hole: Dick with his tripod folded so that it looked like a fishing pole and I with the theodolite that resembled a bucket of worms.

I asked where we were going to set up for our sights.

"On top of that hill over there," Dick answered.

"That hill" looked like a mountain and "over there" must have been a good three miles. It took us two hours to reach the peak.

We were sweating like draft horses and, when we stopped to rest, began to get chilled in our wet clothing. We had committed the usual sin of wearing too many garments. It had been cold on the ship; but after our walk, with the sun bearing down on the rocks, we had perspired freely. If we stayed in our wet clothes we would remain cold unless we kept exercising. There was no alternative but to strip and let the cold air dry everything. So, we danced around in the nude after laying our clothing out on the rocks. Within fifteen minutes it was dry and we stopped dancing. Dick set up the theodolite and began his round of sights. I recorded his readings and logged the exact time of each observation.

Just standing there recording sight after sight got boring, and I was still cold. Between sights (there must be at least fifteen minutes between them to make them worth while) we would hunch down in the lee of the rocks and smoke a cigarette. By the time Dick worked out each observation it was time for another one. Tomorrow, he informed me, we would lay out a base line and cut in the bearings of the other islands.

After our walk over the slippery granite, my feet were sore. On our return to the ship, when I sat down to dinner in the wardroom I discovered that they were not the only sore spots on my anatomy. That rock had been hard where Dick was shooting the sun!

The base line did not take long to establish the following day. Dick asked me to go over to the next island with markers and set them up on the highest hills, where he would take bearings and plot them in. I had been taking star sights and sun lines since I first went to sea, but this was my first experience of applying celestial navigation to survey work.

I stuck a sandwich in my pocket and caught the next boat. The coxswain dropped me off at the island. It was a peculiar feeling to be alone on a piece of rock and realize that I was the first man ever to stand there. Alone, the vastness of the area is overwhelming. There is true beauty in desolation. The silence was awesome, and I envisioned the millions of years of winds and snows that had weathered the granite on which I stood.

In the dim past these rocks were etched by forces that were hard for me to comprehend. Ages of fine snow had eroded the face of the boulders that lay in the path of the prevailing winds. Heat absorbed by the stone had melted snow that ran off, taking minute fractions of the rock face with it. Talk about nature in the raw, I thought, these rocks have never even been scratched by a wild animal sharpening his claws!

I climbed the highest hill and set up the marker. I piled stones about the base of the marker and then led out the triangular strips of canvas and anchored the lines in other piles of rock. In the distance, on his island, Dick bent over his theodolite, and I could picture myself in the view-finder of his instrument. Instinctively, I waved, but he was apparently too absorbed to notice. I picked up the other canvas marker and made my way to the next hill.

Planes had been flying over the area taking aerial pho-tographs, and I could see our amphibian, a mere speck in the sky above me. A helicopter swooped down to a flat spot near by and gently settled to the earth. A figure got out and made his way toward me, climbing over the big boul-ders as he came. The chopper thundered into the air, and I was alone with my unexpected guest.

It was Chet Knowles, chief engineer of the *Burton Island,* and this was his first time ashore in the Antarctic. I was glad to have his company but wondered if we had enough food between us for a midday snack.

"Did you bring any food, Chester?"

"Who wants food?" he asked, and dug deep down into a large leather coat to hold up a fifth of whisky he had been hoarding for several months.

Naturally I shared my sandwich.

We must have resembled a well-known advertisement that shows athletes, explorers, and sportsmen imbibing after a particularly good day of danger and excitement. From our high seat we could see the panorama of islands and the Antarctic continent gleaming white to the south.

The rocky surface of the islands was abrupt. They rose steeply from the water and assumed rounded, unusual shapes, as if some phantom giant had dropped a handful of large pebbles as he walked past.

This area had promise as a site for a future base, we felt. It was on solid rock and was accessible from the sea. It also afforded access to the continent. The islands extended in rows. Any one, adjoining the ice of the continent, would make an excellent base site.

Land plants were few and very small. Only three species of moss and algae could be found in the puddles of water and the moist cracks in the rocks. The abundant plankton life of the sea was in evidence at the water line of the rocky beaches and at the water level of the icebergs floating in the distance.

Chet and I spent the rest of the day waiting for a boat to pick us up and take us back to the ship.

Our work completed, both ships once more sailed in open water. Our destination was the Ross Sea and a revisit to Little America. Our route would take us near the area where we thought the Japanese whaling fleet was working. Their radio signals were very strong, and after some insisting they gave us their position.

We arranged a rendezvous and extended a dinner invitation to the U.S. Army representative aboard. One officer was assigned by General MacArthur to each Japanese whaler to assure compliance with international whaling rules. The date was set for January 25.

Fog was all around us that day. Our own foghorns moaned a protest against the dampness. We had reduced our speed to four knots because we knew other ships were in the vicinity.

Frank Dawley and I watched the radarscope for signs of other vessels. Time dragged as we slowly inched our way southward for the meeting. We didn't want to be surprised by a small "killer" boat from the whaler crossing our bow. Every whaling fleet has several of these small craft that chase and kill the whales. They mark the carcasses with a flag for visibility and for identification of the crew who made the kill.

After their day's hunt is completed the killer boats return and tow the whales to the factory ship, where the mammoth bodies are rendered.

I don't know the Japanese expression, but in Yankee language the factory ships "use every part except the squeal." Of course whales don't squeal, but the crew renders everything much in the manner of a large packing house rendering beef or pork. There is a large market in Japan for whale meat and its by-products.

Pips appeared on the radarscope, and we changed course to close the contacts. They were icebergs. We returned to our original course and closed other contacts. More icebergs. We knew that the whaling fleet was nearby because we had seen a number of dead whales floating past with their flags waving.

To save time we asked the *Hashidate Maru*, the large factory ship, to send "MO's" (an international homing signal of two dashes, pause, three dashes, long pause, two dashes, three dashes again and again) on a known radio frequency. We could follow the bearings when the signals were picked up by our radio direction finder. Soon the RDF showed the long dah dah, dah dah dah. Our course looked good, and we continued.

We skirted more icebergs and proceeded slowly until

the starboard lookout shouted that he had seen a ship. The fog was thinning, and we saw the stern of a large vessel off the bow. We read her name, which was printed in large letters on the fantail, *Todotsu Maru*. The Japanese must have *two* large ships in the area!

We hailed the *Todotsu* but received only vacant stares from the men on deck. Slowly we turned away and headed for another contact. A second large ship came into view, and we read *Yokaku Maru* on her stern. Just how many ships did the Japanese have here? we wondered.

Beyond the *Yokaku* lay the *Hashidate Maru*, and we closed until we could see men waving from her decks.

The *Burton Island* lowered a boat, which went to the *Hashidate* and returned with three men. They climbed the Jacob's ladder and introduced themselves to the task force commander and the captain.

Representing their respective governments as inspectors for the International Whaling Commission, one was an American, another an Australian and the third a Norwegian.

I asked Colonel Winston, the American, if they made the Japanese throw back the small ones; but I suppose it was a poor joke after his year at sea. He failed to see the humor.

The trio were immaculately dressed, but they brought an odor that was hard to live with. After many months aboard the factory ship, their clothes had absorbed the pungent stench of whale oil. Their shoes were soaked in the liquid, and we laughed at their predicament.

Dinner was a complete success. They hadn't seen much variety in the Japanese diet and they pounced on the steaks like starved men. The baked Alaska was the *pièce de résistance,* and they couldn't overcome their surprise at finding a ship serving such a dish while cruising the Antarctic.

After the courtesy call had been returned by Commanders Ketchum and McDonald, fog settled on us again and we began to feel our way slowly northward. We were clear of the whaling fleet, and the cold air smelled clean once more.

Frank Dawley and I agreed that we could have *smelled* our way to them and saved the electricity we had wasted by using radar and RDF.

We sailed in open water all the way to McMurdo Sound. Mount Erebus, a towering volcano, overshadowed the Sound and the western Ross Sea. Its slopes of white stretched up 13,000 feet, and a light wisp of smoke that looked like a cloud streamed from the crater at the summit. With all the exploration that has been done in Antarctica, Mount Erebus is still the only known active volcano.

We landed a survey party on Ross Island. The group of men encountered bad weather and failed to get sights, but that didn't matter too much because this was one of the few areas in the Antarctic that had been charted accurately. Dr. Apfel managed to collect his rock samples, so the stop was not a complete washout.

Ross Island was discovered by Captain Robert Falcon Scott in 1902. He named it for Sir James Clark Ross. Almost everything in the area bears Ross's name. There are the Ross Ice Shelf, the Ross Sea, and Ross Island. The Ross Sea is a large embayment of the Pacific Ocean which reaches deep into the Antarctic continent, causing the contour line of the continent to resemble a giant comma.

We steamed eastward, still in open water, and parallel

to the towering ramparts of the Ross Ice Shelf. As with the Shackleton Shelf, sea action had undercut the lower edge and formed caves near the water line.

The *Burton Island* and *Edisto* nosed around the west cape of the Bay of Whales. High on the shelf east of the bay we could see Tent City, the camp that had been built during Operation Highjump the year before.

To the right and south was the radio tower of Little America, built by Admiral Byrd in 1929. Buried in the snow were buildings, stores, and machines that had been left for possible use by whaling ships in emergencies.

Some of the equipment had been there since 1929, but most of it for only one year. Our mission was to dig out selected items for testing. We particularly wanted to start the engines and check the condition of the airplanes and the automotive equipment.

Captain Buck Boyd headed this project, and it was his lot to establish a weasel trail from the ship's mooring site to the base.

Buck was an Antarctic veteran. He had accompanied Admiral Byrd on various expeditions as a machinist. In everyone's opinion, including mine, he had no peers when it came to fixing something. Once I saw him out of his element when the main rotor blade of a helicopter needed balancing.

Normally this is a job for experienced personnel and is never attempted in the field. But if we couldn't get the blade into operating condition we would lose the services of a helicopter.

Buck took the blade into the mess hall of the *Burton Island*, the only place sheltered and large enough for his work. By moving half-dollar pieces back and forth along

[41]

the blade he quickly determined the point of imperfection and repaired it.

Buck had been from Little America to the Rockefeller Mountains, two hundred miles east, numerous times on the Byrd expeditions. He knew the area thoroughly.

The ice shelf is always in movement. The east and west capes of the Bay of Whales were closing like large pincers and the bay ice was hummocked and rafted.

Tidal action always causes cracks at the junction of the bay ice and the high shelf. Before permitting any men over such treacherous ice, Buck had to select and mark a safe trail. Weasels towing sleds and carrying men would make the three miles over the trail he blazed to the site of Little America.

On one occasion Buck bridged a pressure ridge with oil drums. He cut ice with an axe to cover the drums and make the road level.

Access from the sea-level bay ice up to the fifty-foot-high shelf was obtained by a natural snow ramp. The ramp angle was about thirty degrees, and at the top was the ever-present terminal crevasse caused by tidal action. Buck filled that crevasse, and once the weasels reached the ice shelf the going was as smooth as on the bay ice. Soon loaded sleds were being towed into Little America.

Buck was on home grounds. He knew just where to dig to find any peace of equipment, no matter how long or how deep it had been buried.

Large-tracked vehicles were exposed first. They had been buried a year and subjected to temperatures in the minus seventies. Batteries were tested and found to be in excellent condition. They still maintained a specific gravity of 1.150 and would turn the starting motors. Enough snow was removed to expose the cooling fans and allow a 50 per cent solution of antifreeze to be poured into the first engine's cooling system. It cranked.

A weasel was dug out and started. Then came the apple of Buck's eye—his "little red tractor" that had carried him so many miles during the 1939 Byrd expedition. After the tractor was uncovered, Buck got into the seat, kicked the starter, and drove it out of the deep hole.

Other equipment was disinterred and found to be in excellent condition. Rust was conspicuously absent. Engines of the buried Skytrain aircraft were exposed and started. We could have flown the planes had we had time.

The food was edible, and on the stove in Little America was the remainder of an unfinished meal. All it needed was warming to be palatable and nourishing.

Admiral Byrd had recommended for years that the Antarctic would make an excellent storehouse for surplus food in years of plenty. Here was proof of his theory.

Our inspection completed, we departed the Ross Sea and steamed eastward to see how Finn Ronne and his party were getting along at Marguerite Bay on the Palmer Peninsula, where they had wintered and his ship, the *Port of Beaumont,* was still icebound in the bay.

The Palmer Peninsula stretches northward and nearly touches the tip of Cape Horn. The United States, Chile, Argentina, and Great Britain have occupied bases on this peninsula.

The United States has never made a claim to Antarctic territory, but it has never recognized a claim by another nation. What we call the Palmer Peninsula (sighted first by Nat Palmer, a New Englander) is called O'Higgins Land by the Chileans. To the Argentines it is San Martin Land

and Britons have named it Graham Land.

The *Port of Beaumont* was separated from open water by five miles of hard bay ice which was so thick that we saw absolutely no hope for the little ship to extricate herself. If we could not break her out, it was possible that she would be there indefinitely.

Burton Island and *Edisto* began to battle the ice that wedged the prisoner fast. It was a doubly ticklish job; the ice was thick, and we did not dare force a heavy floe against the *Beaumont*'s hull with too much pressure. The object was to break the ice in such a way that we would open a wedge simultaneously on either side of the beset craft. Her hull and frames might have been strained by the severe temperatures and pressures during the winter night, we reasoned, and any sudden pressure against her hull now might mean the end of the tiny ship.

While we cracked ice toward the *Beaumont,* men from the icebreakers were sent aboard her to make repairs to her engine, rudder, and radio equipment. I didn't pay any attention at the time, but the man sent over to put the *Beaumont*'s radio equipment in operation was Chief Petty Officer Owen Perry who, as one of Dufek's Volunteers in later years, would play an indispensable and dramatic part in Operation Deep Freeze.

Our tactics were successful, for *Beaumont* survived the ice breaking and we dragged her to open water.

Finn Ronne thanked Commander Ketchum for his assistance as the *Burton Island* retrieved her tow line from his ship.

The Second Antarctic Development Project (Operation Windmill) was complete. We had established sufficient ground control stations for the accurate charting of a great many areas. We had determined that Bunger's Oasis was more imaginary than real. The data we had collected on vehicles that had been exposed to severe cold would furnish valuable planning information to the military establishment.

Every man aboard was now at least an "expert" after one trip. Ketchum had advanced to the rank of "authority" on completion of his second trip, and Frank Dawley became an "old explorer"—a distinction reserved for those who have made three or more trips to the Antarctic.

OPERATION DEEP FREEZE

I _____

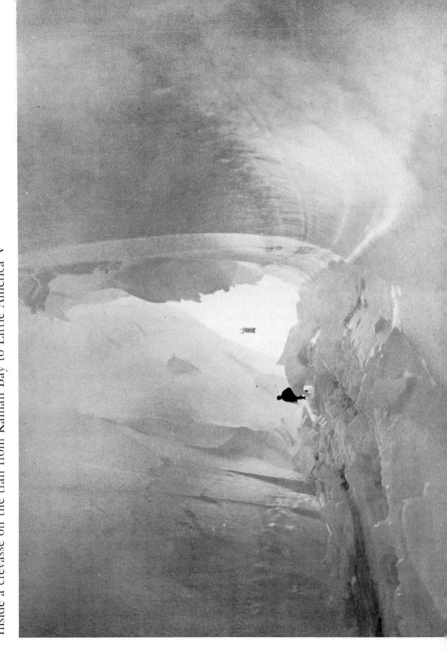

Inside a crevasse on the trail from Kainan Bay to Little America V

A view down the partially completed main tunnel at Little America V

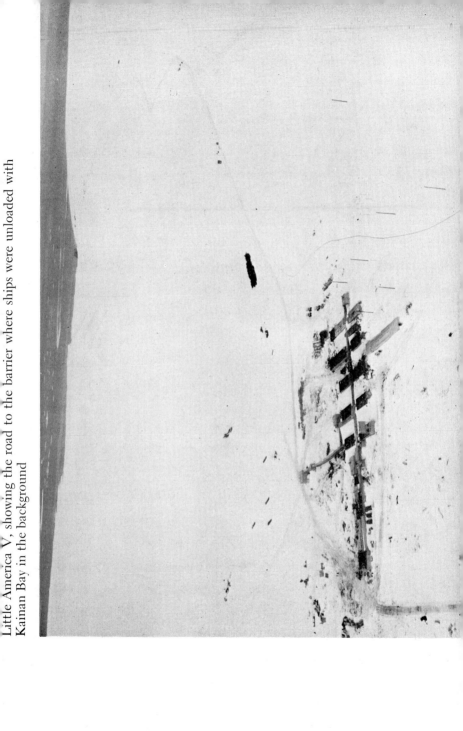

Little America V, showing the road to the barrier where ships were unloaded with Kainan Bay in the background

Seabees plant an American flag and grave marker 110 miles from Little America V where Max R. Kiel, CD 2, died March 5, 1956, when his tractor plunged into a crevasse.

Non-wintering-over personnel prepare to leave Little America V for big America.

The bow of the USS *Glacier* nosed into the ice barrier at Vincennes Bay during a
sixty m.p.h. blizzard.

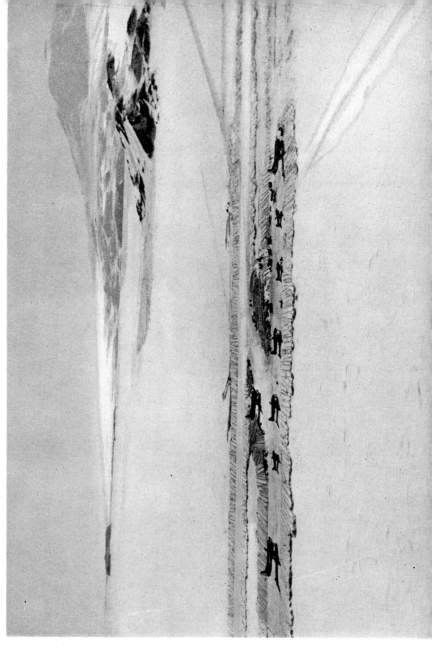

Planes of Air Force Development Squadron Six and the 18th Air Force on the parking mat at Naval Air Facility, McMurdo Sound, with Mount Erebus in background

Lt. Condit, USN, gives last rites to a victim of a P2V crash on the sea ice runway at Williams Air Operating Facility, McMurdo Sound.

5 ———————————

I BECAME executive officer of the *Burton Island* and made two trips to the Arctic before my initial tour of polar work ended. Then, as if I hadn't been separated frequently enough from my family, I was ordered back to destroyers. I had command of the U.S.S. *Shelton* for two years when the call went out for Deep Freeze volunteers.

My old friend Gerald Ketchum, now a captain, was deputy task force commander when I reported to Washington in the spring of 1955 as one of Dufek's Volunteers.

Typical of Ketchum, his office had no door, and I just walked in.

"Hi, Paul, glad to see you finally made it," he said. Such is the Navy. After six years in different parts of the world we picked up where we left off.

"Meet Captain Charles Thomas, chief of staff."

I shook hands with a silver-haired, pink-cheeked Coast Guard captain who would have appeared much more at home as a professor in a college classroom than he did in his military uniform planning an Antarctic expedition. Looks can be deceptive, for I knew he was one of the world's foremost experts on ice matters. As skipper of the icebreaker *Northwind* during Operation Highjump Captain Thomas had performed valiant service by rescuing trapped cargo ships.

Captain Ketchum pointed out my office and told me to get "squared away" before he introduced me to the staff.

I was to share the office of Commander Verne "Penny"

Pendergraft, an aviator.

"Your desk's over there. The coffee pot is in the next room," Penny greeted me.

"What's the size of this job, Penny?" I asked.

"It looks big, and it is big," he said. "We are to support American scientists in the Antarctic during the International Geophysical Year."

Penny talked with a big cigar in the corner of his mouth. My weight had slipped over the two-hundred-pound mark, but Penny outweighed me.

My orders said I would be assistant chief of staff for ship operations. Now was as good a time as any to get started, so I poured myself a cup of coffee and sat down.

Penny stacked file folders on my desk until I could hardly see over them. Somewhere in this maze of paper must be the answer to what we were going to do, I figured. If the operation was to be as big as its advance paper work I'd never see my family again.

I opened the top folder and began reading:

"The purpose of this operation is to implement the program in the Antarctic by conducting operations during the period of 1954–1959 and subsequent thereto as directed by competent authority.* Such operations will include:

"(1) Supplying logistic support for the U.S. National Committee—International Geophysical Year.

"(2) Conducting special scientific projects as requested by agencies of the government, within the capabilities of the forces assigned. This would include such projects as meteorology, hydrography, and oceanography.

"(3) Establishing stations in the Antarctic as directed by competent authority, in support of United States scien-

* The icebreaker *Atka* had made a solo reconnaissance in 1954–55.

tists in the area.

"(4) Conducting other scientific investigation."

There it was—four simple-appearing charges, clearly spelled out, yet they were fraught with hidden danger. In spite of the cost, the operation would overshadow any accomplishment made by any nation in the ageless history of the Antarctic. I felt a tingle of excitement at being associated with such a sweeping program of exploration.

Spelled out, the charter orders meant the world was getting ready for another Polar Year, the largest one of all.

As a result of my interest in Polar matters during the past several years, I had read extensively on the subject. The last Polar Year was 1932 and, according to my memory, the next one should be held in 1982. Here the time interval of fifty years was being cut in half. Was my memory failing? I made a mental note to check the facts as soon as I got a chance.

I went back into Captain Ketchum's office and we began our round of introductions, an old custom in the Navy. The Captain was as practical in this as he was in all other matters. We walked to the various departmental offices in the staff building, rather than wait for a formal conference.

I shook hands with Commander Charley Snay, the communicator, Commander Bob Hartmann, the public information officer, and then walked into the photography room to find Lieutenant Commander Charley Shirley, an old friend, back as photographic officer.

"I still think, Charley, that you photographers are a waste of time and money. If I had my way we would give everyone a Brownie camera, two rolls of film, and get more and better pictures."

[51]

His assistants choked over their coffee, but Charley knew me. "Now don't give me any trouble, Paul," he said.

I met Commander John Mirabito, the aerologist, and when we had refilled our coffee cups Captain Ketchum took me back into his office. I had a lot of questions, and I knew he had the answers.

Before we could start, Chief Petty Officer Owen Perry, my old friend from the *Burton Island*, walked in. He was the man who had repaired the radio equipment on Finn Ronne's ship, and he would prove to be a mainstay on the ice during Operation Deep Freeze.

As Perry left, a supply officer walked in. "Meet Don Kent, Paul. He is our logistics officer and controls all of our money."

When Kent had left, Ketchum and I both remembered Pete Petersen of Task Force 39. "Where is Pete?" Ketchum asked me.

"Somewhere in the Smithsonian, but I don't know what he is doing."

We laughed over the bags of Antarctic rock Pete was going to sell for a dollar, and we felt sure Pete had followed through with his wild idea.

The grin left Ketchum's face.

"We have a big show this year, Paul, and you have a tough job as Ship Operations. We are going to build two bases this year and five next year. One of these will be directly on the South Pole."

Again my nerves tingled. The Pole had been reached by only two parties in history. Amundsen made it in December, 1911, and Scott followed a few weeks later, only to die on his return journey.

Now we were going to build a base there. It never

occurred to me to inquire *why* we were going to do it; the mere fact that we were was enough.

"The chief of staff for operations is Captain Douglas Cordiner, but he won't report in for a few weeks. In the meantime you will work directly under Captain Thomas," Ketchum said.

Captain Thomas swiveled around in his chair and presented me with a stack of papers.

"Read these. This is a rough draft of the Operation Plan. We have to get the plan into shape and to the printers for mailing in July."

"Yes, sir."

I took the papers and returned to my desk. It was early April, and July seemed a long way off.

Captain Thomas's draft of the Operation Plan looked good.

"The general scope of this operation contemplates the execution of a plan outlining minimum floating forces to support the International Geophysical Year on the Antarctic Continent and to gain further knowledge of the geography of Antarctica and hydrography of contiguous waters.

"The general plan calls for the establishment of the following stations and having them ready for occupancy by scientific and supporting personnel required for scientific projects by about January 1, 1957:

"Little America Station at Little America (Kainan Bay) or vicinity.

"Byrd Station at Latitude 80 South, Longitude 120 West.

"Pole Station at South Pole.

"Weddell Sea Station, Weddell Sea.

"Knox Coast Station, Knox Coast.

"Cape Adare Station, Cape Adare.

"In addition, and in order to support operations of heavy aircraft in Antarctica, an air operating facility will be established in the vicinity of the Ross Ice Shelf.

"As soon as practicable after operations commence in the Antarctic," the plan continued, "six planes will be flown from South Island, New Zealand, to the air operating facility at McMurdo Sound. If bay ice lends itself to wheeled landing, two other planes will accompany the flight.

"These aircraft will be supported during the flight by all vessels of the task force. They will be augmented by four small ski planes and three helicopters which will be ferried in by ships to the Antarctic.

"The Little America station and the air operating facility will be installed as soon as possible after penetration of the bay ice in 1955–56 season.

"A fuel farm will be built at Little America and an airstrip suitable for taking off and landing ski planes will be constructed.

"*Little America will construct and support Byrd Station by tractor train operation.*"

I gave this sentence no more than a passing glance, at the time. It struck me as being a rather difficult job—sledging the hundreds of tons of cargo needed to build a station across some six hundred miles of treacherous ice. But, you will recall, I was "Ship Operations" and could afford to sympathize with the joker who drew the ice-blazing job, without getting excited. I had no inkling at that early date how the cards would fall when the hand was dealt two years later.

"The air operating facility will serve Pole Station

which must be constructed during the Antarctic spring, 1956, and supported by airlift. This lift calls for aircraft and approximately 80 men to be provided by the United States Air Force. At McMurdo Sound, wind-swept bay ice lends itself to aircraft operations. However, if possible, a snow-compacted runway will be constructed as an anchor to windward in the event the bay ice breaks up and goes out. The bay ice will be tested during the presence of task force vessels in the Antarctic."

That will be a famous first, I thought, operating heavy aircraft from sea ice.

The plan continued:

"In the event bay ice does not lend itself to use by heavy aircraft, the flight of four-engine planes from New Zealand will be deferred until after the snow-compacted runway is completed.

"In October 1956, two Douglas Skymasters and Air Force cargo planes will fly to Antarctica. The former will map while the latter will provide airlift of materials to Pole Station."

Now there's some interesting reading, I thought. If Scott died just getting back from the Pole, who were we to build a base there? And by airlift!

I laid the plan aside and reflected on its magnitude. The entire operation must be tied together like a time table, I knew; but I also knew that time schedules in the Antarctic are the next thing to useless.

I told Captain Thomas the plan looked good to me but I thought the schedule would be impossible to meet because of unknown weather and ice conditions.

"You're right, Paul," he said. "A schedule is just a general guide in the Antarctic. We will all be working toward the same goals and play it by ear."

"What happened to your hair?" a booming voice from behind me asked. I felt a strong hand touch the bald spot on top of my head.

Captain Thomas and Captain Ketchum got to their feet, and I followed suit. The voice and hand belonged to Captain George Dufek. I recognized him from his pictures: hardy, handsome, with steel-gray hair and friendly eyes, all man from head to toe.

"Glad to have you with us, Frazier!"

How did he know who I was?

Captain Ketchum made the introductions and Captain Dufek's warm friendly manner made me like him immediately. His face was brown from the sun, and it contrasted pleasantly with his graying hair. (As crisis merged into crisis, I would watch his hair turn from steel-gray to snow-white during Operation Deep Freeze.) Combat decorations covered his left breast. He wore the dolphins of a submariner and the wings of an aviator.

"Thank you, Commodore," I mumbled.

"Commodore" is a term used in the Navy to address anyone in a broad command position who does not hold flag rank.

Captain Dufek disappeared into his office.

"The Captain doesn't like to be called Commodore, Paul," Captain Ketchum told me. "He will retire shortly, and there is a bill in Congress to authorize him to remain in command of the task force when he retires. He will be retired as a rear admiral because of his combat awards. He will be recalled to active duty the day after his retirement."

"Yes, sir," I said. That was a fine way to start out on a new job with a new boss. Already I had goofed.

My first chore was to get ships ordered to the Task Force. On the basis of estimated tonnages of cargo we would need two cargo ships, one tanker, and two icebreakers.

The Commander in Chief of the Atlantic Fleet assigned us the *Glacier*, our newest and biggest icebreaker; the *Edisto*, my old friend from Task Force 39; the tanker *Nespelen*; the amphibious cargo ship *Arneb*; and the attack cargo ship *Wyandot*.

Cargo for the operation was being assembled at the Construction Battalion Center in Davisville, Rhode Island. Within a few months it became obvious that our original estimate was too small. When the tonnages were established a few weeks later we asked for another cargo ship and an additional icebreaker. We got the *Greenville Victory* and the Coast Guard icebreaker *Eastwind*.

Specially designed buildings had been ordered. They were of lightweight construction and used aluminum beams with plywood panels. Each section fitted together with a key locking device for speed in construction. When completed, such a hut could stand up against 100-knot winds and minus-100-degree temperatures.

In a cold-chamber test, Herb Whitney, commander of the construction battalion, learned that a building could be assembled in three hours with the thermostat set at fifty degrees below zero.

The contract for snow tractors was awarded to the Caterpillar Tractor Company. Soon large and small tractors began arriving at Davisville on flatcars. Their wide, low-ground-pressure tracks made them look larger than they were, so that a thirty-seven-ton D-8 model was a behemoth to behold. Tracks on that model were fifty-four inches wide. Width of the tracks, coupled with special alloys used in their cab construction, meant that the thirty-seven-ton tractor would exert only sixty pounds pressure per square inch on the ice.

One day I called Davisville to confirm a sailing date with Herb Whitney. He sounded extremely worried, and I asked the reason.

"I'm short one D-8 Caterpillar tractor!"

"You mean somebody stole a 37-ton Cat?"

"I don't think so," he said; "but all we ordered have been shipped from Peoria, and I'm still short one here."

I didn't dare let him hear me laugh over the telephone, but I could envision an Alexander Botts story in the making. The setting was perfect: A caterpillar tractor stolen from a railroad siding, whisked off to a hide-away, repainted, and used to demonstrate a competitive brand.

"We're still looking," Herb said. "I'll let you know how we make out."

Two days later I had occasion to call him again. He had found the big Cat.

"Where was it—on a used-car lot?"

"No. At Sears and Roebuck!"

"Now take it easy, Herb," I said. "I'm a customer of Sears, and I never thought they'd steal a D-8 tractor from the Navy!"

"They didn't steal it. The freight car got on the wrong siding and ended up at Sears. One of my chief petty officers saw it while he was shopping."

Hurricanes enveloped the United States east coast. Building panels and beams en route by truck overturned in one storm. The panels were special-order and there was not time to replace them. They were retrieved, a bit weather-beaten, and delivered to Davisville for loading on the ships.

Every time I thought our plans were set somebody would assign us another mission, and we would have to review our capabilities. Usually we needed more men, more ships, or more money to meet the order. Logistics was a serious problem because our rule-of-thumb guide was that, for every man left on the ice, we had to transport nine tons of cargo to support him. This included buildings, food, and clothing.

Antarctica is one of the few places on earth that offer absolutely no chance of foraging or purchasing supplies. You take along what you need, or do without.

When Navy and Air Force fliers made known their fuel requirements we realized that the storage facilities for aviation gasoline we had anticipated would be woefully inadequate. Somehow we had to get more gasoline storage, and the manufacturer's lead time between order and delivery on large tanks was such that they could not possibly be manufactured soon enough unless we resorted to an expensive crash program. We were reluctant to spend that much money, and so we began to seek a cheaper solution.

Captain Ketchum called me into his office.

"Paul, what do you know about YOG's?"

"A YOG is a small, self-propelled gasoline tanker. When I was port director at Saipan, I had six of them operating out of the port," I said.

He asked if one could go to the Antarctic under its own power.

"During the demobilization at the end of World War II, I was sailing them from Saipan to Pearl Harbor under escort. They didn't encounter any rough weather on those trips, but I have seen them ride out typhoons at sea off Saipan."

"But," he asked, "do you think they could be frozen in and stand the pressure of the ice?"

"I think so. Remember the *Port of Beaumont* was only slightly damaged when we dug her out of the ice after a winter night in 1948."

"Put some study on it, and let me know where the best place would be to freeze it in," he ordered.

I told him I thought there was a sheltered spot in Winter Quarters Bay where Captain Scott had frozen the *Discovery* in for the winter, and a ship should be able to survive the winter there.

"Well, see if you can find us a YOG," Captain Thomas said.

"There is one hitch, Captain," I cautioned. "At the best speed, a YOG will have to leave about two weeks from now to get there, and we won't have any ships to serve as escorts for at least a month."

"Look into towing it then," he said. "I remember seeing one in Iceland that had been towed there."

I learned from the Service Force commander that tows of YOG's were usually made at seven knots, with the barges only half loaded so they would have plenty of freeboard to protect them against heavy seas washing over their bows.

A suitable YOG was located in the mothball (reserve) fleet at Seattle, Washington, and I went to look at it. We wanted to keep over-all costs to a minimum and didn't want to ask for more men than we needed for the job at hand. I had to see, first, that the barge was seaworthy and, secondly, what would be a minimum crew.

A request for volunteers went out to the various commands that comprised Task Force 43. Lieutenant "Dusty" Blades, a flier, volunteered to skipper the barge. His crew consisted of aviation ratings and Seabees for the most part. The Admiral's steward was chosen as cook.

After minor repairs the barge was towed to Panama, where the rest of its crew would go aboard. It would be towed from Panama to New Zealand by the *Edisto* and from New Zealand into the Antarctic.

Still the scientists and other government agencies made demands for services. Each time we accepted a new mission it meant a new requirement for gasoline because, for some reason, it seemed everything anybody wanted required the use of an airplane.

We had decided to gamble with one YOG, so now we asked for a second one. We got the one Captain Thomas had seen in Iceland several years before. The icebreaker *Glacier* was ordered to tow it from Norfolk to the Antarctic.

Now, I thought, if we could just get out of the country before somebody else wanted us to carry out another mission, we would be all right.

It seemed that if one more job was piled on us I would find myself asking for the entire Atlantic Fleet.

With enough bottoms assigned to handle our cargo and fuel, I was given the onerous job of creating space for the passengers. Each ship had just so many bunks, some in staterooms and some in the crew's living compartments. The staterooms were of course more comfortable and offered more privacy, so they were in greatest demand.

The passenger totals were still growing, and I could see much anguish when Mister Civilian was assigned to a living space that didn't suit him. This required protocol!

The problem was resolved when I found a directive

that had been put out by the Military Sea Transportation Service which spelled out a comparison between civil service grades and military ranks. The biggest problem such an arrangement created was that there were so many high-level state servants the junior officers would find themselves billeted in the crew's compartments.

A Department of Defense directive said press correspondents were to be given the simulated rank of lieutenant commander. Well, I reasoned, we already have lieutenant commanders sleeping in the crew's compartments, so let the fourth estate growl.

I had spent a number of years in destroyers where conditions were really crowded, and the hassle about berthing failed to excite me. I had long ago arrived at a philosophy which helped me make many decisions: No matter what the decision is, half the people won't like it. If you should decide the other way, the other half won't like it. No matter which decision you make, you are sure to be wrong, so the hell with it.

As the summer wore on I played more and more golf with Lieutenant Homer Flippen, the Task Force construction officer. He shot in the middle eighties, about twenty strokes better than I. But even with our differences in scores we enjoyed relaxing at the Army-Navy Country Club in Washington. We made secret plans to build a golf course in the Antarctic.

One day Don Kent, the logistics officer who was now also personal aide to Admiral Dufek, joined us. (Dufek had reached the statutory retirement category when he completed thirty years service June 30. He was promoted to Real Admiral on his retirement and was recalled to active duty the next day to retain command of Task Force Forty-three.)

"Don," I asked, "can you please get the Admiral to stop inviting every soul in Washington to go to the Antarctic? They all accept, you know, and bunk space is about gone. It's going to be embarrassing to me to say we don't have any more room; but it will be more embarrassing to the Admiral to find himself a bedfellow."

"I know, Paul. You might mention it to the Admiral next time you see him."

Don sank his putt, and I missed mine. I just hoped we would leave soon.

I took the movement orders in for Admiral Dufek to sign. The *Edisto* and *Glacier* were to sail from Boston October 30. The *Eastwind* would sail thirty days later, after she returned from operations in the Arctic. We held some concern for the happiness of the *Eastwind*'s crew; sailing for the Antarctic one month after returning from the Arctic.

Coast Guard Headquarters in Washington canvassed the *Eastwind*'s crew to see who wanted to go. It was amazing; they all volunteered.

The supply ships *Wyandot*, *Arneb*, and *Greenville Victory* would sail from Norfolk November 13. They would be preceded by the tanker *Nespelen*, scheduled to sail November 6. The YOG's would be picked up by the icebreakers at Norfolk and Panama.

Throughout the fitting-out period we had been besieged with suggestions, some sound and some crackpot. One crank predicted the end of the world during the International Geophysical Year, and another told us it was "useless to continue." One wanted to fly over the South Pole in a Tuxedo because it had never been done before. A young lady thought she and her boy friend should be a part of the wintering-over party; another just wanted to go along because she thought she would be useful.

Flags from organizations throughout the world were stacked in my Washington office. They would be duly flown over the pole and returned to adorn a historical spot on somebody's wall. It seemed the only flag not included was the Higginsville, Missouri, High School Band flag. I resolved to speak to the bandmaster the next time I went home.

We were swamped with philatelic mail. We had anticipated a few hundred bags but had to handle thousands. An attempt had been made to restrict each collector to five covers, but the limits were badly abused. At sailing time we had to stack mailbags in the cabs of snow tractors loaded on the weather decks of the cargo ships. There was no other place to put them.

Bob Hartmann, the public information officer, had his problems too. We had reserved twelve spaces for news correspondents, but Bob received only three acceptances. The *New York Times* sent Bernie Kalb; the Associated Press, Saul Pett; and the National Broadcasting Company, Bill Hartigan. After these three uninhibited individuals filed their first stories, Bob was besieged with requests. Before the operation ended fifteen members of the working press were busy on the ice.

Space had run out, and money was becoming critically short; but the Admiral kept saying, "There's always room for one more." Somehow, however, everything we needed got off to the Antarctic. The departing ships left nothing on the dock and Don Kent still had some money up his sleeve for "emergency" items.

Diplomatic clearances were requested for each foreign port the ships and planes would visit, but they did not come through until a few days prior to our departure. As Ship Operations, I began to wonder what the hell I would do if some nation said "No!"

6 ——————————————

BANDS played and crowds waved to the ships bound for the ice. As we left the receding coast line behind us, it was a tremendous relief to be quietly at sea after the hectic months of office frustration.

The *Glacier* and *Edisto* made remarkable time, towing the YOG's at the rate of fourteen knots instead of the expected seven knots. We had had to load the small barges to capacity with fuel, and they rode low in the water. Meals, water, and other necessities were passed by high-line to them under tow.

Aboard the flagship *Arneb*, as on all the ships, officers, crew, and passengers busied themselves in drills to be ready to handle any emergency. Motivation for iceberg collision drills is a bit difficult in tropical waters, but we rammed many an imaginary berg on the way and successfully shored each "hole" in our hull.

On the eve of Thanksgiving I looked aft to see a pair of red lace undies flying abreast of the Admiral's two-star flag on the after yardarm. The Pollywogs were at work. Next day we would be crossing the equator, and all first-timers would be initiated into the royal domain of Neptunus Rex. They would, through initiation, advance from lowly Pollywogs to honored Shellbacks. But on the eve of initiation, the Pollywogs were having their last fling.

Hips made sore by flogging and faces burned by gun grease during the initiation were salved somewhat by a fine Thanksgiving dinner. Then we resumed our eternal preparation for the day we would encounter ice.

Captain Ketchum had already arrived in New Zealand with the icebreakers, and he wired that the Admiral was expected to attend a great number of state and civic dinners on arrival. His message was followed by others from the embassy. The Admiral was in for a busy four days, socially.

Then we encountered a bad storm which put us two days behind schedule.

Rather than create an international *faux pas* by arriving too late for his own parties, the Admiral directed one of the planes (already in New Zealand) to meet the flagship off Chatham Island.

When the seaplane arrived, the seas were too choppy for it to land. The craft began circling overhead while the pilot spoke to the ship's duty officer by radio. Meantime, a boat had been lowered into the water to carry the Admiral to the plane when it landed.

Dr. Rochus Vogt, the young German scientist who was responsible for operating the cosmic ray equipment on the *Arneb*, calmly watched the proceedings from his spot on the navigation bridge

The Admiral's baggage had been placed on the ship's forecastle to be lowered into the boat when it came abreast of the ship. A rain began to fall, drenching his gear and every man on deck.

The boat came alongside the quarterdeck, and Admiral Dufek climbed down into it. Soon the coxswain signaled frantically that the boat had developed a leak, and that he was coming back alongside to be taken quickly out of the water.

At this tense moment, the boatswain's mate of the watch began to test out the ship's loudspeaker equipment,

[67]

unaware of the confusion that already existed.

"Testing One Two Three Four Five Four Three Two . . ." he droned over every circuit. Behind him could be heard the anxious voice of the airplane pilot asking for instructions.

Still Dr. Vogt watched and listened from the bridge.

Finally the plane was told to land in the lee of Chatham Island. A small boat came out from the island to pick up Admiral Dufek. The flagship lay to until the Admiral's plane was airborne.

After the confusion died down the German scientist shook his head, turned to the chief quartermaster, and asked:

"How did you guys ever win the war?"

The *Arneb* and *Wyandot* entered Port Lyttelton, New Zealand, December 13. Huge crowds thronged the docks to welcome us. Our send-off from America had been a small private party in comparison to the thousands who greeted us in New Zealand.

"Good on you, Yank," shouted the warm-hearted throngs. Smiling, friendly faces peered up from the docks at smiling, friendly faces peering down. Liberty commenced as soon as the gangway was in place.

The *Wyandot* was tied up across the dock from the flagship. *Eastwind* was on the other side of the slip, and the YOG's hugged the fuel pier. *Greenville Victory* and *Nespelen* were beyond the *Wyandot*. The icebreakers *Glacier* and *Edisto* had already sailed to make their reconnaissance of the ice pack and to learn whether the sea ice at McMurdo Sound was strong enough to receive the large wheeled airplanes.

We were besieged with invitations to dance, hunt,

fish, and visit. Within minutes after liberty call the docks were almost empty. American sailors had been accepted into New Zealand society.

The Admiral called a conference for midafternoon. He arrived on the pier and was cheered by the remaining people. Side boys saluted smartly as he was piped over the side and made his way to the wardroom, where the various commanding officers were gathered.

"The weather doesn't look good yet for the fly-in, but when I get word from Captain Ketchum that things are ready at McMurdo and the weather is right we'll be off.

"Meantime, grant as much liberty as possible. Just remember, we may leave on short notice. I hope we can stay here about four days; but time is precious, and our stay could very well be cut short.

"Now let's hear from the rest of you."

Each commanding officer expressed his readiness to sail or fly as the case might be. Staff members reported final arrangements had been completed.

The telephone rang. "A helicopter has just crashed in the harbor near the *Eastwind!*"

"Anyone hurt?" the Admiral asked.

"No one injured."

"Continue with your reports, gentlemen. We can strike one helicopter from the force."

The conference continued. If the duty sections could not handle the situation they had no business being aboard ships headed for the Antarctic.

Lieutenant Commander Glenn "Judge" Lathrop was the pilot of the helicopter. As he took off from the pier alongside the *Greenville Victory* his rear rotor failed and the helicopter began to spin. There was some danger of it flying apart under these conditions, and "Judge" didn't want to hurt the bystanders, hundreds of whom had gathered to watch him take off. He dumped the helicopter into the water and, with his plane captain, bobbed to the surface from a depth of thirty feet. The helicopter was later recovered and returned to the United States for repairs.

Frequent reports kept the Admiral advised as to the status of the crew and the salvage of the plane. Everything was handled as it should be, calmly, efficiently.

"That completes the conference, gentlemen. Thank you very much for coming," he said.

This was the first emergency in which I saw Admiral Dufek, and I was immensely pleased. He had never raised his voice; never appeared worried. He had witnessed crashes before, and, although they could never become routine, he had such command of himself you would have thought someone had spilled a cup of coffee.

I realized then why no one under his command ever let him down. He expected you to do your duty, and you did it to the best of your ability. Others in the same situation might have rushed to the scene and created confusion. He expected the situation to be handled in his best interests, and it was.

Don Kent and I accompanied the Admiral on a round of social calls that night and checked into our hotel. We looked over the messages and retired. There would be no flying tomorrow. A low-pressure area was approaching from south of the Tasman Sea, and John Mirabito predicted head winds for any flights launched. Flight would be marginal with no winds, possible with tail winds, but hopeless if head winds prevailed.

There were more parties and more invitations the next

day. I accepted all invitations, as did the Admiral. Our host at the final party of the day showed us some of the trout in his deep freeze, and the sight immediately captured the Admiral's imagination. He is a born fisherman, and he snapped up an invitation to go fishing the next morning.

Periodically the Admiral asked me to call John Mirabito for the latest weather report. Things were looking better to John, but it was still too early to be sure.

"Perhaps after twenty-four hours conditions will be favorable. Certainly within the next seventy-two hours," he said.

Pendergraft and I shared a hotel room. Captain Thomas occupied a room on one side of us, and Captain Cordiner on the other. About four A.M. my phone rang, and I struggled into a sitting position to answer it.

"Paul, this is Don Kent. Captain Ketchum has just informed the Admiral by radio that everything is ready for the fly-in. The Admiral wants a conference in forty-five minutes in his suite at the hotel. Will you round up the staff?"

This was my first experience at middle-of-the-night conferences, but it wasn't to be my last. I went about waking up staff officers.

I knocked on Captain Thomas's door, then Captain Cordiner's. Penny was on the phone calling those who were staying at other hotels, alerting them to stand by if needed by the Admiral. I never did figure out where he thought they would be going at four A.M.

My knocking awoke the rest of the hotel guests, and the manager came up in his night dress to see what we crazy Yanks were up to at this hour.

I told him, and he ordered morning tea for the conference. In a few minutes we were assembled in the Admiral's suite, sipping tea in various stages of dishabille.

Admiral Dufek and Don Kent walked in, fully decked out in uniform and looking fresh as daisies.

"Ketchum is all ready for the fly-in. The ice is level for the planes to land, and John Mirabito says the weather is going to be good within seventy-two hours. I want to get under way at noon today so the ships will be on their radio picket stations. How about it?"

Penny was shore patrol officer. He spoke first.

"We have a lot of men on two-day passes, Admiral."

"Call them back."

The Admiral looked at me.

"Ships are ready."

He looked at Captain Cordiner.

"Penny can call the radio stations and ask them to announce for everyone to return aboard and that the ships are getting under way at noon."

He turned to Captain Thomas. "Ready?"

"Ready."

"Let's get going," he said.

We packed our bags and returned aboard ship. Christchurch's two radio stations broadcast the call for Yanks to return to their ships, and men began pouring into Port Lyttelton. Some arrived on bicycles, some walked, and friends drove others back to their ships. We received a call from two hundred miles away. A Seabee was being rushed to the ship pony express style from one friend in one town to another friend in another town. He made it back on time.

The docks were filled again when the ships backed out at the stroke of noon. Every man had returned to his ship, and we were all lined up at quarters for the departure. As the last line was cast off, one man sailed his white hat into the crowd and in about thirty seconds every white hat visible on deck was flying through the air to the cheering throng below.

I had never seen anything like that departure, but was told that all New Zealand farewells, since Captain Scott first sailed from that beautiful country, were just like this.

Eastwind, Arneb, Wyandot, Greenville Victory, and *Nespelen* rounded Godley Head and proceeded to their ocean stations on the flight line between the southern tip of New Zealand and Cape Adare, Antarctica. *Eastwind* towed one of the YOG's.

Within a few hours the Admiral would have to make a profound decision—whether to launch aircraft for the first flight in history from an outside land mass into the Antarctic.

7

WE raced to take stations between New Zealand and McMurdo Sound for the first intercontinental flight to Antarctica. The ships would be posted along the flight path at 250-mile intervals to send radio beacon signals to help the airplane navigators. They would also be in position to aid any pilot who was forced to ditch in the ocean.

The *Glacier*, which had penetrated the ice pack with the *Edisto* to determine that the sea ice at McMurdo Sound was safe for heavy airplanes, would be on station in the ice pack. *Edisto* would remain at the landing site to vector the planes in.

Once the aircraft landed, we would rendezvous off Scott Island and be convoyed through the pack by the *Glacier*.

Weather reports indicated December 21 would be the best date for the fly-in. If the planes could not be launched that day, Mirabito feared it would be seven days before weather fronts shifted in such a way that tail winds would again prevail.

While we steamed to take up our picket stations, Captain Ketchum's men marked off the landing strip on the sea ice. They attached red flags to bamboo poles and stuck them into the snow on either side of the natural runway. When the approach of aircraft became imminent, men would augment the trail flags by holding smoke signals along the sides of the runway. Either the trail flags or the smoke signals would make good landmarks on the clean white ice if the weather was good; but if a white-out rolled in *Edisto*'s radio homing signal would be the pilots' only comfort in making blind landings.

A shift in the weather prompted Admiral Dufek to set the launching date up twenty-four hours. At six P.M. December 19 he ordered the airplanes dispatched at dawn the next day.

The long-range Skymasters and Neptunes would fly from Christchurch while the shorter-ranged Skytrains and Albatrosses would take every advantage of the New Zealand geography by leaving from Taeri Field at Dunedin, the southernmost airport.

Aboard the *Arneb* it was hard for us to visualize the pilots' preparations for their historic flight across two thousand miles of water and ice from New Zealand to Antarctica. On previous expeditions, aircraft had been carried in aboard ships or flown in from carriers operating just outside the ice pack. We knew the airplanes would be loaded to capacity with gasoline and would have to blast off with JATO bottles (jet-assist) to get airborne.

We rolled gently in a westerly swell. Weather reports came in every hour, and Mirabito plotted them on a chart. A low-pressure front was developing to the northwest, but John didn't think it would cross the flight line until after the planes had passed.

There were no reporting stations between the line of ships and Australia, and this left large blank areas. Eighteen stations in the southern hemisphere were expected to send weather reports, but only thirteen could be received. Of the thirteen, only one lay in the general direction from which we most desired reports.

Penny Pendergraft, Charlie Snay, and I shared a cabin

aboard the *Arneb*. Charlie would be busy taking care of communications, so Penny and I relieved each other every four hours as flag duty officer.

Sleep became more difficult as we waited for the message telling us the first plane had left New Zealand. Mirabito didn't sleep at all. Neither did Snay.

Charlie broke us out of our bunks at five A.M., December 20.

"The first one has taken off!"

He showed Penny and me the message: "P2V number 122466 departed Harewood at 0456 GMT. Expected time of arrival McMurdo 1913. Time enroute 14 point three hours. Pilots Torbert and Hawkes."

That's leadership, I mused. Trigger Hawkes, the Navy's top polar aviator, had planned the fly-in, and he was in the first flight making sure it was safe for those who followed. To his credit, he was flying as copilot to Lieutenant Commander John Torbert, a fine pilot but a relative newcomer to polar flying.

Penny dressed and went to his station in the plotting room. I followed in a few minutes with a cup of coffee.

Admiral Dufek and Captain Cordiner had been in the plotting room all night. The room was littered with full ash trays and empty cups.

It was dark, but the displays of the route of the aircraft on the lighted Plexiglas boards provided enough light for us to see our way around.

A man bent over the radarscope, watching each sweep of the cursor as it circled. It was much too early to expect any aircraft in our vicinity, but I could sense the tension.

"P2V 122465 departed Harewood 0512. ETA McMurdo 1912. Time enroute 14 hours. Pilot Entrikin."

Two planes separated by sixteen minutes were now airborne. A plotter filled in the departure information on the status board with a grease pencil and filed the message.

"UF 142428 departed Taeri 0646. ETA McMurdo 1806. Time enroute 11 point 3. Pilot Sparks." Then, a few minutes later: "R4D 12418 departed Taeri 0647. ETA McMurdo 2010. Time enroute 13 point 4. Pilot Shinn."

(Ten months later the same aircraft and pilot would electrify the world when they landed Admiral Dufek at the geographic South Pole.)

"R4D 17274 departed Taeri 0653. ETA McMurdo 2039. Time enroute 13 point 8. Pilot Frankiewicz."

"UF 142429 departed Taeri 0646. ETA McMurdo 1806. Time enroute 10 point 9. Pilot Graham."

What were they doing at Taeri, launching with a catapult? All the departures were logged on the status board, and the messages filed. Penny sent for a steward to clean up the dirty coffee cups. The steward brought more coffee and cigarettes for the Admiral. He had been smoking my cigarettes, and he pushed his fresh pack to me. I slid them into my pocket.

Now reports were coming in from the *Greenville Victory* that the planes were being passed from her to the *Wyandot* for control. It would be some time before control would be turned over to the *Arneb*.

"Do you have the watch, Paul?" the Admiral asked.

"No, sir."

"Let's go eat."

I followed him down to the flag mess for breakfast. Normally there were eight of us for meals in the flag mess, but that morning there were only four. I finished my breakfast and went back to air plot. The Admiral came up when the departure report of the Skymasters was filed.

"R5D 56505 departed Harewood 0815. ETA Mc-Murdo 2215. Pilot Kolp."

"R5D 56528 departed Harewood 0830. ETA Mc-Murdo 2200. Pilot Jorda."

We laughed at 528 challenging 505 to a race; leaving fifteen minutes late and listing his arrival time fifteen minutes early.

So far, so good, I thought. All planes were airborne.

Nespelen turned control of the first plane over to *Arneb*, and we dashed to the flying bridge to see if we could spot the first P2V. There was an overcast which prevented us from seeing the plane, but we talked to the pilot by radio as our radar operator verified his course and position.

The two Albatross tri-phibians reported headwinds and turned back to Dunedin shortly before reaching their point of no return. Equipped with wheels, skis, and pontoons, they offered too much resistance to the head winds. The R4D's plugged along, struggling against the same head winds. It became obvious they could not make McMurdo Sound with sufficient gasoline reserve, but still they came on. Admiral Dufek spoke.

"Order them back to New Zealand, Doug."

Captain Cordiner picked up the microphone. "274—418: You are *ordered* to return to base! Acknowledge!"

The replies were desultory but both pilots turned back, deeply disappointed.

The R5D's were under our control now, and we went to the bridge again to see if we could spot them. One was a fleck of silver fleeting through the clouds above us. The other was at a lower altitude and dipped his wings as he passed over.

Arneb turned control of the airplanes over to the *Glacier*, and we breathed a sigh of relief. As soon as we got word that the UF's and R4D's had landed safely in New Zealand we could order the ships to rendezvous.

Six hours later we learned they had arrived in New Zealand, and the rendezvous order was sent.

Ships headed for Scott Island, and a weather front moved in as if a curtain had been pulled down on the last act of a drama. *Arneb* skirted the limits of the ice pack plotting hydrographic information as we waited for the other vessels to catch up. Dull routine, this waiting, but I had learned patience many years before.

We received word the P2V's and R5D's had landed safely at McMurdo just before a white-out moved in. The pilots and crewmen would live a very austere life until the ships were escorted through the pack with supplies to build permanent bases. They would pitch tents for shelter and subsist on survival rations while they waited.

I returned to my books for the two days it took the *Arneb* to reach Scott Island. In Washington I had been too busy making plans for Deep Freeze I to grasp fully the scope of the International Geophysical Year.

I had known this was to be the third "Polar Year" and the first had been held in 1882. It amazed me now to read how it all started.

The original idea of international scientific investigation in the polar areas is credited to a Lieutenant Weyprecht of the Austrian Navy, a veteran of two Arctic expeditions. He was dissatisfied with their scientific results and what he termed "exploration for exploration's sake." He gave his concept of exploring at a meeting of the German Scientific and Medical Association at Gratz in

1875 and stressed scientific research rather than exploration as the objective of future expeditions. He also emphasized that geographical discoveries were of value only when they extended the field of scientific inquiry.

Bismarck liked the young officer's ideas and appointed a commission to study them.

The commission also liked Weyprecht's ideas of locating observation stations where they could best serve the scientific discipline to be studied, permitting the observations to be analyzed while they were being conducted over a period of time.

They thought it most important that investigations be conducted by cooperation of many nations because of the high cost of staging expeditions.

Count Wilczek helped Weyprecht plan his presentations for the International Meteorological Congress, but the meeting was delayed by the Russo-Turkish War. It finally met at Rome in 1877, and Weyprecht's plan was favorably received.

General participation was a requirement, and the congress called a conference to meet at Hamburg later in the year and discuss the details. It was their combined opinion that "these observations will be of the highest importance in developing meteorology and in extending our knowledge of terrestrial magnetism."

Eight countries sent delegates to the convention, and three others sent word that they were in favor of the plan. Twelve stations were agreed upon, and four of these were to be in the Antarctic.

Rules for observation of the scientific disciplines were formed, and it was agreed that no nation should be bound to the agreement until at least eight stations were assured.

The front view of a crevasse detector operating with the advance party blazing a trail over the 644 miles from Little America V to Byrd Station

Interior view of a crevasse in the area where the Ross Ice Barrier meets Rockefeller Plateau. The advance party spent eighteen days covering 7½ miles here, making a trail safe for the largest tractor train ever assembled in Antarctica.

A surface view of a crevasse that nearly swallowed a tractor and driver on the trail to Byrd Station

A Navy R4D beside a fuel cache on the Byrd Station trail, 250 miles southeast of Little America V. Planes flew fuel out for use by the tractor train.

The following year, Austria-Hungary, Denmark, France, Germany, Italy, the Netherlands, Norway, Russia, and Sweden sent delegates to a conference in Berne.

The minimum of eight stations was assured, and the year 1882 designated as the first International Polar Scientific Year. Further agreement was reached that a similar polar year should be held every fifty years along the same lines as the first, with as many nations as possible taking part. The second International Polar Scientific Year was held in 1932–33.

In 1950, at the home of Dr. J. A. Van Allen in Washington, Dr. L. V. Berkner suggested during a social gathering that perhaps a scientific year every fifty years was too infrequent. In the second Polar Scientific Year science had made great strides. Shouldn't scientific investigation on a global scale be conducted every twenty-five years to bring basic research up to date with the latest scientific advances?

Doctors Sydney Chapman, Wallace Joyce, S. F. Singer, and E. H. Vestine agreed. Their idea was carried to the International Council of Scientific Unions, where it was accepted. There would be an International Geophysical Year in 1957–58, and the earth would be covered with thousands of scientific stations.

There would be circles around the world from pole to pole at three different longitudes, and other circles around the world in the Arctic, on the equator, and in the Antarctic. Hundreds of nations would participate, and many would have one or more stations in the Antarctic. Six thousand stations would engage in basic scientific investigation. Doctors Chapman and Berkner were appointed Chairman and Vice Chairman for the Geophysical Year.

I felt proud that in my position I could be a small part

of the Navy's support to our scientists' efforts in the Antarctic. Admiral Dufek had been told where the men of science wanted their stations, with Task Force 43 as his working instrument. His job was to put them there. As a member of his staff I had definite responsibility toward the success of the venture.

I put the book down, turned off the light, and let the gently rolling ship rock me to sleep. I could tell by the foghorn that it was foggy outside.

The messenger woke me at three-thirty to tell me I had the watch. I climbed from my bunk, dressed, and quietly poured myself a cup of coffee in the flag mess. The Admiral was asleep in the next room, and I could hear his breathing as I drank my coffee. That watch was quiet, as were succeeding ones.

"Iceberg sighted off the port bow," a voice blared from the *Arneb*'s public address speakers. I could visualize the camera fans dashing below for their cameras and falling over themselves getting topside to photograph the berg. Frank Dawley and the *Burton Island* came to my mind. I wondered if the *Arneb*'s exec would possess the Solomon-type wisdom Frank Dawley had used in the event an argument came up as to whether the berg was officially sighted first by radar or by lookout.

I must be growing old, it seemed. I drank another cup of coffee and let the novices waste their film. But after pouring cream into the coffee I too edged over to the side of the bridge to see the berg. It could have been the same scrawny one I had seen seven years before, weathered and beaten, not much to look at; but it was ice.

We picked up Scott Island on radar, and the *Arneb*

took station in an area southeast of the island. The surrounding waters were divided so each ship could steer in circles within its own sector without ramming another ship while we waited for the more distant ones to keep their rendezvous.

Wyandot reported in by radio and was assigned her sector. *Nespelen* called and received hers. We waited for the *Greenville Victory* for what seemed hours. Finally she radioed to report twenty radar contacts, any one of which could be Scott Island. She asked if we had her on our radarscope.

Our scope was so littered with icebergs we could not be sure. Without a fix on Scott Island, *Greenville Victory* could not reach her sector satisfactorily. We knew she was close because her voice radio signal was very strong. An hour passed, and each time we thought we had her located it turned out to be another iceberg.

The thought came to me that Fred Robinson, the aerologist of Task Force 39, had told me how amazing it was that the low-pressure areas in the Antarctic were small and intense as compared to those in the lower latitudes.

I called John Mirabito and asked whether we couldn't locate *Greenville Victory*'s position by weather reports. He was willing to give my crazy scheme a try, so we got barometer readings and wind directions from each ship in the vicinity of Scott Island.

Captain Duchowski, master of the *Greenville Victory*, must have thought me insane when I told him what I was attempting to do. But he cooperated, as did all the other ships.

When Mirabito had plotted all their weather reports he looked up and said, "She should be bearing zero three seven, ten miles from Scott Island."

I called Captain Duchowski again and directed him to steer two one seven degrees true, the reciprocal of his bearing from the island. "You have ten miles to go, Captain," I told him with false assurance.

Captain Duchowski was an experienced seaman in the polar regions and knew how to handle his ship. We all marveled at his ice seamanship.

Our radar operator watched his radarscope in the northeast quadrant. "I have a moving target here, Commander."

The *Greenville Victory* was assigned to her sector, and she verified the fact that she had Scott Island on her radar.

A few hours later we tried the same procedure with the *Glacier*, but it didn't work. We spent four hours getting the *Glacier* into contact with Scott Island.

"It's all right, John," I told Mirabito; "We're batting .500 anyway."

8 _____

ADMIRAL DUFEK, Captain Thomas, and I transferred to the *Glacier* in one of the *Arneb*'s small boats. When we climbed over the side Admiral Byrd and Commander Pat Maher, the *Glacier*'s captain, greeted us. The admirals disappeared into the cabin for a conference while Captain Thomas, Maher, and I went to the bridge to get the convoy under way.

The column for penetrating the ice would be *Glacier*, followed closely by the tanker *Nespelen*, then *Greenville Victory*, *Arneb*, and *Wyandot*. *Eastwind*, with her YOG in tow, had not yet arrived. She could make her own way through the pack.

Not knowing *Glacier*'s capability, I was hesitant. We started off at five knots. In a few minutes it became obvious that we could go much faster with safety, so I increased speed to nine knots.

Ice flew in all directions from the powerful *Glacier*'s bow; but the wake was clear, and the convoy steamed in an ice-free lane southwest for McMurdo Sound.

Every few hours Admiral Dufek, Captain Thomas, or I would scout the ice ahead by helicopter to learn the best route. I marveled at the advances which had been made in polar flight clothing during the years I had been flying helicopter reconnaissance. Only ten years before, Admiral Dufek had crashed on a similar flight and received a cold dunking. He stayed in the water less than four minutes but would have frozen if he had not been rescued when he was.

[85]

Now we wore rubber exposure suits which permitted immersion in cold water for several hours if we crashed.

The suit was difficult to put on because it encased the body completely, except for our face and hands. After a few minutes it became extremely uncomfortable, but no relaxing of safety regulations was permitted.

The Antarctic summer of 1955 was a "light ice" year, and our convoy made its way the entire three hundred miles to McMurdo Sound at an unprecedented average speed of nine knots. *Edisto* had been ordered to join the convoy after the fly-in, but she had to turn back to help rescue survivors when a small Otter plane crashed. Her hospital facilities meant life to two seriously injured men. This left the entire convoy with only one icebreaker. Normally one breaker is required for each three ships, but *Glacier* was up to the task and delivered her charges safely to McMurdo.

When we arrived in the late afternoon of December 26 a conference was called aboard the *Glacier*. Captain Ketchum presented some dismal facts.

The ice was ideal for aircraft operations—so ideal, in fact, it would be extremely difficult to penetrate by the ships destined for McMurdo Sound with supplies to build the air base. He advanced a plan to begin unloading the cargo ships thirty-eight miles out, sending cargo by sledloads while the icebreakers inched their way closer to the base site. The thirty-eight miles was true, point-to-point distance. His estimate proved correct that the tractors, in skirting tidal cracks, might travel up to fifty miles each way.

As soon as *Glacier* had assisted part of the convoy to Little America and broken ice for them, she would return to attack the ice at McMurdo Sound. When *Eastwind*, with her YOG in tow, and *Edisto* arrived, three breakers would work in unison against the hard thick ice of the Sound.

The *Wyandot* and *Nespelen* remained at McMurdo Sound as units of Captain Ketchum's task group while *Glacier* led *Arneb* and *Greenville Victory* to seek out a base site which would become Little America Five.

Aboard *Glacier* we steamed in open water along the face of the Ross Ice Shelf for some four hundred miles, looking for an ideal base location. The *Atka* had reconnoitered the area a year before and reported that the Bay of Whales had calved off and gone to sea, leaving a large, unprotected area with sheer ice cliffs too steep for use in unloading the cargo ships. Admiral Byrd, however, who was sailing on the *Glacier*, still hoped there might be a possibility of locating a berth near the Bay of Whales, scene of four of his precious Little Americas. Sentimentality is a strong factor.

When we reached the Bay of Whales, Little America I, II, and III rested close to the edge of the barrier. Little America IV, which I had visited in 1948, had gone to sea when the barrier calved off. The only means of access to the old camps was by helicopter, so Admiral Byrd had to visit his former camp sites by air.

Somewhere in the Ross Sea, four airplanes were floating around on an unpiloted iceberg; the phantom aircraft carrier of the Antarctic. The planes had been left behind at the conclusion of Operation High Jump.

At Kainan Bay, thirty miles to the east, we found the spot the *Atka* had recommended as a base site. It offered good possibilities, but we continued looking eastward until it became obvious that there was no choice. We returned there and made preparations to unload the cargo ships.

Somehow it seemed a sacrilege to invade the purity of the scene we beheld. Kainan Bay was a horseshoe-shaped indentation in the towering ice shelf. The bay was approximately four miles square, hemmed in at three sides by the barrier. Sea ice which would be used as the initial unloading platform looked deceptively thin in comparison to the barrier's sheer walls that reached a hundred feet up in some places.

We spotted a natural "ramp" of snow that could be used by tractors pulling sledloads of cargo from shipside up to the high barrier. Our first problem was to insure that the ramp was not interlaced with cracks. Such cracks, or crevasses, are the greatest of all hazards to surface travel in the Antarctic because, as often as not, they are covered by safe-looking snow bridges. Before heavy loads can be sent across the ice, a careful check must be made, foot by foot, to see if the snow is substantial enough to hold the weight of the vehicle that will travel over it.

The total distance from shipside to the base site was five miles. Captain Thomas and I felt fortunate, by comparison with the task at McMurdo, that we had such a short haul.

Glacier broke out a small bay in the sea ice so that the ships would be protected from the winds and sea while they were unloaded. Within four hours the mighty icebreaker had carved out her channel and shaved off the jagged ice edges that would otherwise have ruptured the hulls of the cargo ships. Captain Thomas and I moved aboard the *Arneb* to supervise the unloading, and this was to remain our headquarters at Little America for some time.

Greenville Victory and *Arneb* came alongside the ice,

buried their ice anchors (called "dead men" because the anchor or timber is buried), and made ready to discharge cargo.

While the trail blazers explored and marked a safe trail up the ramp to the base site, ships' crews began unloading. First they lowered the tractors and sleds, then the cargo for delivery by sled to the supply dump about two miles away.

On paper that supply dump looked like a good idea. All cargo could be stacked by an intricate identification system there, then dragged up to the base site as it was needed during the period of construction. Yet it was to cause one of the most distressing and dramatic incidents of the first year's operation. Now it seems foolish that we would have ever built a supply dump on sea ice when the barrier was only a mile or so further from the ships. But we did, and we paid dearly for our mistake.

For four days the unloading moved smoothly. Both Captain Thomas and I spent more time on the ice than aboard *Arneb*. Tractors shuttled between ships and the supply dump while other tractors moved between cargo dump and base site. Permanent-type buildings began to take shape on the lonely ice barrier.

Then all hell broke loose.

Storms a thousand miles to the northward began making themselves felt at Kainan Bay. Heavy ground swells began washing the cargo ships against the edge of the ice where they were unloading. The same swells caused the seaward edge of the ice to surge vigorously up and down and calve off in great chunks. The ships could put to sea and ride out the crisis, but several thousands of tons of cargo were still sitting at the sea-ice supply dump. Half our base could fall through in a few hours unless we got it to the barrier immediately.

At once, every available man was ordered to the cargo job. Signalmen abandoned their flag bags and lights; oceanographers put away their nets and bathythermographs; photographers "secured" their photo labs; even the coffee urns in the ships' chief petty officers' quarters were allowed to grow cold as every man buckled down to the task of manhandling cargo. Only the medics and cooks were excused.

I remember working, straining at a crowbar to dump cargo from the sleds at the camp sites so the sleds could be rushed back to the bay ice for another load. On my shift were a chief yeoman, a chief journalist, a civilian press correspondent, and several other clerical ratings who I knew had not done a day's manual labor for many years. They thrived on the work. I saw the Admiral himself "heaving around" on the cargo.

Four hours after the last crate was safely on the barrier, northerly swells broke up the ice that had been the supply dump. Ships slipped their anchors and raced seaward to avoid being crushed.

When it got calm enough for the vessels to return, the bay was only half as large as when we had started. Nature had broken and washed away more ice in one storm than a thousand breakers could have broken in concerted action. But one good purpose was served; the distance from shipside to base site was appreciably reduced.

Greenville Victory still had large tractors aboard, and it was imperative that these be unloaded as quickly as possible. The machines were on deck and blocked a hatch which was loaded with cargo.

The storm had left a jagged ice spur which would have been dangerous to the *Greenville Victory*'s hull. We decided to blast it off with dynamite because the *Glacier* was away on a hydrographic mission. She had left Little America soon after creating the cargo ships' berths.

Shaped charges of TNT were set off in a line designed to cut the spur free. It stood fast. More shaped charges were used, but they only created small holes in the ice. Below decks it sounded like some giant banging the ship's side with a large maul. Each time a blast was detonated the crew would run topside to see if any damage had been done.

Captain Duchowski expressed fear to Herb Whitney, the Seabee commander who was doing the blasting, that his ship could not stand the concussion, and Herb promised to pay for any necessary repairs out of his own pocket. He didn't have to pay off; but neither did he blast away the twelve-foot-thick spur. I decided that if the ice could stand that blasting it could stand the weight of a thirty-seven-ton tractor.

Admiral Dufek watched as the first vehicle was lowered over the side gently onto the spur. Gingerly, the slings were loosened and removed. The tractor's engine had been started before it left the ship. A Seabee wearing a life preserver and a safety line climbed into the cab and drove it to safer ice.

The tough spur remained until *Greenville Victory* was completely unloaded. It stood the weight of seven tractors and fifteen twenty-four-pound TNT charges. You can't tell about ice, I realized.

Admirals Byrd and Dufek placed Little America in commission January 4 when *Glacier* returned from her oceanographic mission. The base was a long way from being completed, but Admiral Dufek wanted to release *Glacier* so she could help Ketchum's force at McMurdo Sound.

Captain Ketchum was having serious trouble getting his cargo to Hut Point. The long hauls of cargo across the fifty-mile ice course was wearing down the tractors and crews alike. The Wind class icebreakers *Edisto* and *Eastwind* made pitifully slow progress against the tough, hard, old sea ice which had been standing so long its salt content had drained downward. Salt-free, the ice had the tensile strength of a high-grade plastic and the brittleness of a cutting diamond.

Immediately after the commissioning ceremonies at Little America, *Glacier* was dispatched to give assistance to her companions. It had been a comfort to us to know that *Glacier* was near by and could come to our rescue if anything happened to the cargo ships, but we knew she was needed worse at McMurdo Sound. She turned the tide completely, accomplishing in a few days what had completely stopped the two Wind class icebreakers.

But before *Glacier* completed the channel to Hut Point, tragedy struck the expedition. Tractor driver Dick Williams was cautiously edging his heavy vehicle across a tidal crack that had been bridged when the ice gave way. Because of his engine's noise he could not hear the ice breaking, or the shouts of his friends; so the machine plunged into a hundred fathoms of icy water, carrying him to a swift, frigid death.

Rather than chance the loss of further drivers, Captain Ketchum recalled all tractors to the ships until the icebreakers could open a channel closer to Hut Point.

With *Glacier* setting the pace, the icebreakers mastered the seemingly unconquerable ice. *Glacier* was larger, heavier than, and three times as powerful as the older craft. Within a few days a channel was broken to within five miles of Hut Point.

But you can't beat nature in the Antarctic. The ice which had given two icebreakers such a hard time had finally been mastered by a more powerful ship. Now the winds shifted in such a manner as to trap the crushed ice in the channel *Glacier* had opened. Blowing from the north, the wind held it almost as firmly in place as if it had not been broken.

Now, Captain Ketchum proved his mettle. If the cargo ships cannot penetrate the ice-clogged channel, he reasoned, we will transfer cargo to the icebreakers and let them ferry it to the base site until the wind shifts. The task was difficult, slow, and involved back-breaking labor, but it was successful.

Ketchum had delivered the goods; but I learned by reading his radio reports at Little America that he had broken the cardinal rule of *patience*. By ordering the ice-breakers to plow through the ice at maximum power, they had done such a thorough job that they almost wrecked the sea-ice landing strip where the airplanes were parked.

As soon as the broken ice drifted free, permitting tidal action to work against the seaward edge of the sea ice, great cracks began to develop. Some of them inched up to the very parking strip where the airplanes stood.

Nine vital reconnaissance flights were scheduled for the long-ranged R5D and P2V airplanes. The plan said these flights would be extended over the Antarctic summer season of some six weeks to three months.

But with their landing strip crumbling while only a third of these missions had been completed, the aviators were hard pressed to complete their assignments. They taxied up to the ships, refueled alongside, and took to the air. All nine flights, one of them the longest in Antarctic history, were completed by the middle of January, and the planes were evacuated to New Zealand.

At Little America we marveled at Ketchum's luck in mastering the ice and at the aviators' good fortune in completing their task. But our job was no picnic in comparison.

During the crucial battle to get the ships unloaded, I spent more time on the ice than I did on the ship. After the first few days I began to notice that a large number of the Seabees were not returning for meals or to sleep. I decided to investigate. We had made arrangements to deliver food to the base site, and we had installed the galley equipment in the first hut to be completed; but sleeping accommodations were not yet built. "Big Ed" Edwards, a former lumberjack from Washington state, was leaving the ship with a sledload of cargo. He slowed momentarily to shift gears, and I jumped aboard his tractor to ride with him into Little America.

Even at the slow pace of three miles an hour the ride was hair-raising. Conversation was impossible, so Big Ed just pointed at anything to which he wanted to call my attention.

At the top of the ramp a crevasse stretched on either side of the trail. The portion under the trail had been filled, but after every fifth or sixth tractor passed it required refilling. Our heavy vehicle lurched sickeningly as it jarred across the depressions in the route.

I pointed like mad but Big Ed, cigarette hanging from

his mouth, did not appear concerned. He had made the trip so many times it was becoming habit with him to pass over the dangerous spot.

In low gear the tractor slowly hauled the sleds up the hill of ice. Another vehicle edged toward us on the trail, leveling the ruts that had been cut by the sleds. It pulled to one side as we passed, and Ed pointed to the driver, then back along the trail, indicating that his one-finger signal meant the crevasse at the top of the ramp needed filling. I wanted to ask him what two fingers would have meant, but he couldn't have heard me even if I had shouted to the top of my voice.

Ahead, I could see two tractors with sleds just going into camp. Behind us another edged up over the top of the ramp.

We rolled smoothly down the hill into "crevasse valley" and onto the filled bridge. It was like crossing Grand Canyon on a plank. The span was just wide enough for one vehicle. A sign at either edge marked its width and proclaimed.

"This road was built by Fat Max and a Dirty Bearded Texan."

At the time, these words provoked a chuckle. In months to come, however, both Fat Max Kiel and the Dirty Bearded Texan, Ed Gardiner, would become very real quantities in my life, even though I had no inkling of them now as Big Ed and I rode through Crevasse Valley.

From the right side of the enclosed cab I could look down into a seventy-five-foot hole. Ice has a peculiar way of changing colors when it is cracked. At the top it is white. A few feet down it is a beautiful shade of sky-blue. As the depth increases, the blue gets progressively darker. The bottom of the fissure into which I found myself staring was black. Big Ed flicked his cigarette into the chasm on his side of the bridge and lighted another. The tractor rumbled across.

There was a long line of unloaded sleds as our machine groaned up the last hill and into Little America. Big Ed parked his sleds at the end of the line and maneuvered over to the maintenance shack.

Another sign greeted us:

"Little America Gas and Oil. Courteous Service. Clean rest rooms. Proprietor, Chief Moore."

The big chief petty officer greeted Big Ed. "Whad dya want?"

"Fill 'er up. Check the oil."

Big Ed and I walked over to a wind-blown tent which was more of a canvas lean-to.

"Whatcha got for lunch, Burleson?" Ed asked, as he wrapped his hands around a cup of coffee. I stand six feet tall, but I had to look up at him. Our clothes made us appear like giants, but I was a midget compared to Big Ed. His hands did to that cup of coffee what Goose Tatum's hands do to a basketball when the Harlem Globetrotters come to town.

Bill Burleson was a first-rate mechanic. He doubled by serving as cook on one shift. At various times while inspecting the trail I had seen a weasel bouncing from rut to rut on its way to repair a tractor. It seemed that Burleson was always the man chosen to perform the repair. Yet each time I got to Little America I would stop at the "Little America Drive-in" and Burleson would be cooking stew, soup, coffee, or some other concoction.

"Do you have a twin brother down here, Burleson?"

"No, sir, just me."

"What's cooking today?"

"Chili. Have some."

I heaped a bowl full and watched the Seabees come over to do the same. The chili was good. Watching the men eat, I got the feeling that I was in a logging camp.

I finished the food and dipped my bowl in a can of boiling water before setting it back on the shelf. Around the cook shack were buildings in various stages of construction. I saw a familiar figure duck into a hut, carrying a hammer.

It was Owen Perry, my old friend from Task Force 39 days. I couldn't imagine what he was doing with a hammer unless he had "flipped" from exasperation and was about to use the tool to destroy his radio transmitters and receivers.

I followed him into the half-finished hut that would soon become Radio Little America. He had all the electronics technicians and radio men doubling as carpenters. Some hammered at wooden panels and cabinets while others led wires to various terminals or shifted equipment around.

"When will you be ready to go on the air, Perry?"

"Commander, I'll tell you, but please don't pass this on. We said we would be up two days from now, but we have been on the air for the past forty-eight hours.

"If the ships knew we were on the air we'd be loaded with traffic. I'd just as soon get things 100 per cent ready before you start snowing us with radio messages!"

He had given me another reason to believe, as Captain Ketchum had said, that Owen Perry was the best electronics man in the Navy.

Empty packing crates littered the room. A tired sailor was asleep in one of them.

"This where you men have been sleeping?"

"Yes, sir. That's my box over there."

The case was marked "Transmitter," but it was empty. Its contents had already been installed.

"Perry, is this fellow's name Ramsden?"

"George Ramsden. He's a first-class radio man. He's been up all night for the past few days."

"I realize that, but was he ever on board the destroyer *Mansfield* for duty?"

Ramsden and I had talked about the Antarctic in 1949 when I was his exec. Here, six years later, he had volunteered to winter over. I was glad to see an old friend, but I didn't wake him up. He needed his rest.

I was looking over the supply dump when Lieutenant Don Mehaffey, the supply officer, approached. We are great friends now, but at that time there was no love lost. He was the so-and-so who was not sending the sleds back to the ship fast enough, and, conversely, I was the so-and-so who demanded so many sleds at the ships that their cargo had to be dumped on the ice rather than unloaded in an orderly fashion.

"Commander, the sleds are coming up so fast we can't unload them and stack the material in such a way that we can find it when we need it."

"Don," I said, "you are taking so damn long to unload the sleds we're going to be here for six months. The ice can't last forever, you know."

"I don't care about the ice. All I want is my stores where I can find them. Just look at this lousy mess!"

Boxes were stacked on boxes and there was a mixture

of color codes which confused the issue. These codes looked fine in the operations plan, but they had long since given way to expediency.

"You've got my sympathy, Don, but it's better to have the cargo up here in a mess than to lose it through the bay ice. If that ice goes out, you won't have anything up here to gripe about."

Our battle had run for several days.

"We need more men," he said.

"Damn it, you've got everybody up there but the Admiral's steward already!"

"How about him?"

How about him? The Admiral had gone. His steward, his yeoman, and his messenger were available. So was his flag lieutenant. There must also be some others that could be taken away from other jobs. I couldn't wait to get back to the ship. I called a conference with the department heads.

"Mehaffey needs more men. I've sent every man available to me, and the ship has furnished all it can spare. Starting now, cargo is everybody's business."

The flag lieutenant, George Porter, was given a crew. So was Chester Stout, the flag chief yeoman. Soon Porter's Porters and Stout's Stalwarts began to compete with each other to see who could unload the most sleds in a twelve-hour shift.

Everyone had been working in one of two twelve-hour shifts and the strain was beginning to show, so a twenty-four-hour holiday was declared.

The *Arneb* carried beer for just such an occasion, and the Seabees who would winter over also had beer available.

Football fields and baseball diamonds were marked off

on the ice. I set up a nine-hole golf course, and Captain Thomas and I played one round before we joined the baseball game.

Greenville Victory beat *Arneb* and challenged the Staff. The winners would take on the Seabees in a third game.

Men dressed in parkas and holding cans of beer lined the base lines to watch. The temperature was ten degrees above zero, but the sun beat down on the ice. Some of the participants stripped down to their waists.

A player would hit the ball, then slip toward first base while the fielders slid and fell trying to catch the ball. Penguins entered into the spirit of things and finally broke up the game.

Penguins are naturally curious, so they gather to watch anybody doing anything. A baseball game is paradise to them.

They pass their eggs to each other when one goes to take a bath, catch a fish, or just swim. When they return to their rookery they in turn receive an egg from another penguin if there are enough to go around. More often than not there is a shortage, so Mama or Papa Penguin will nestle anything resembling an egg.

The penguins must have figured we were playing baseball with penguin eggs because suddenly one took off after a long drive to centerfield and beat the fielder to the ball.

She, or he, didn't throw the ball back. She just sat on it, probably thinking it was an egg which had been lost some months before. This stopped the game, but nobody seemed to care. The beer was all gone anyway.

I felt badly that Homer Flippen wasn't there to play

on my golf course, but he was busy at McMurdo Sound helping Captain Ketchum.

Flippen almost got to Little America at that. Danny Slosser, executive officer of the Seabee Battalion, had to return to the States for personal reasons after he had volunteered to winter over. With the job vacant, Admiral Dufek wired Flippen at McMurdo Sound:

"Desire you become executive officer of Battalion and winter over at Little America. You volunteer, don't you?"

Flippen volunteered, but it was later decided that he was needed on the staff in Washington more than at Little America.

Lloyd Beebe, a civilian cameraman for Walt Disney Productions, taught us a lesson at Little America. He carried a heavy camera wherever he went. I feel sure it weighed more than a hundred pounds. He would put on his snowshoes, strap his gear across his back, and proceed to the point of interest.

To the "old explorers" among us, snowshoes are out of place in the Antarctic. The well-dressed explorer must wear skis, even though he doesn't know how to ski. One day I doubled with laughter when I saw Beebe walking *backward* on his snowshoes, photographing a couple of "old explorers" walking toward him on skis. They were laboring forward, and he was gracefully keeping in front of them—in reverse.

By the middle of January we had most of the cargo off the ships, and the tons we had dumped on the barrier were fast being converted into an orderly camp. Then Nature moved against us. I was returning from the base site where I had been unraveling some bottleneck that delayed the rapid unloading of the ships when the message came:

"RETURN TO THE SHIP. THE ICE IS BREAKING UP ALONG-SIDE."

Captain Larry Smythe of the *Arneb*, where we were still berthed when not occupied ashore, wasn't telling me a thing. The ice was breaking up where Captain Thomas and I stood. We ran toward the vessel as fast as we could in our heavy clothing.

The ship loomed out of the fog. Between us and our goal I glimpsed the shadow of a widening crack. I could hear the ice opening. It sounded very much like a man forcing a dry concrete slab apart with a crowbar—a grinding crunch followed by a squeaking-door sound, which sent cold chills up my spine.

I stopped briefly to wave the tractors back up to the safety of the barrier, then sprinted toward the ship. I knew that the tractors had a much better chance of reaching the barrier safely than they did of racing for the vessel at three miles an hour to be hoisted aboard.

Captain Thomas and I jumped a four-foot crack and grabbed the gangway. It was moving up and down as the ship rolled in the swell. We hastened to pull ourselves up before we got dunked in the water.

The *Arneb* moved to sea. It had been a close call, but time was all we had. I felt grateful that *Greenville* had been completely unloaded two days previously and released from the area.

By the next day the swells calmed considerably, so *Arneb* returned to the ice edge and again began discharging cargo.

Twelve hours later the swells again got the best of the ice and *Arneb* was chased seaward again. This time she had to fight her way through heavy broken slabs of ice that had once been the outer edge of Kainan Bay.

The storm continued in its full fury for two days as we sat off the embayment wondering if there would be any ice left to unload cargo on. The wind shifted January 22, blowing all the broken ice to sea. Less than half a mile of it remained in Kainan Bay.

Remooring, *Arneb* discharged her remaining cargo in thirty-six hours. The short turn-around distance between the ship and the base now made it easy for the tractors to shuttle supplies to the base.

Just as the last sledload reached the safety of the barrier, ground swells destroyed all the remaining bay ice, but we didn't care. All cargo was high and dry on the towering ice shelf. It wasn't stacked neatly, but it was safe.

When the gasoline tank was completed at Little America, the *Nespelen* arrived from McMurdo Sound, escorted by the *Edisto*. *Nespelen* pumped her fuel to the tank and we steamed away from Little America in company, the flagship *Arneb* preceding *Edisto* and *Nespelen*. We would make a final call before heading home, but the base was, for all intent and practice, on its own. We were needed at McMurdo Sound.

9 ——————————————

JACK BURSEY put out from Little America January 14, when we were about halfway through with the unloading. His job was to locate a safe trail some six hundred miles across the ice to the site of Byrd Station, flag that trail for tractor trains to follow with fuel loads, then return to Little America before nightfall in late March.

"Pemmican Jack" Bursey had a lot of qualifications for his job, but we expected too much from him. His mission was doomed to failure before he left Little America. But Jack was never one to quit without trying. He had been in the wintering party with Admiral Byrd's 1929 expedition, and he had returned on each of Admiral Byrd's trips. He was as experienced on the Antarctic ice as any American. As a dog driver with the early expeditions he had spent as many as eighty-three consecutive days on the ice trail.

But we arrived so late in the Antarctic season and experienced such difficulty getting the cargo and vehicles off the ship at Kainan Bay that Bursey was off to a late start—so late, in fact, that he would have to work in haste to blaze the trail and return to Little America on time.

Work stopped momentarily the day Bursey and his seven-man party put out. The chaplain said a prayer, and all hands wished the small party good fortune as they departed in a Sno-cat and two weasels, all pulling sledloads of fuel, food, and such survival items as trail tents, emergency rations, and sleeping bags.

A single-engine Otter airplane would fly support missions to the trail party; and the same plane would fly reconnaissance missions when Bursey's party encountered heavily crevassed regions.

Every quarter-mile the navigation weasel would stop while Jack jabbed a flag in the snow to mark the trail. A tractor train would follow this trail as it laid down fuel caches for the next year's tractor trains, dragging five hundred tons of cargo to build Byrd Station at 80 degrees South, 120 West.

Bursey moved briskly along. Within two days he had reached a crevassed area a hundred twenty miles from Little America.

I flew out in the Otter with Lieutenant Bob Streich to see what the trail party was up against. Bob revved up the plane's engine and taxied over to a gasoline pumping unit mounted on skis at Little America. It seemed strange to see an ordinary, highway-model gasoline tank on the desolate ice wastes with no trucks closer than three thousand miles. When the plane's tanks were filled, Bob lifted two fifty-gallon rubber tanks of additional fuel into the cabin.

Air burped from one of the tanks, and I was sprayed with fuel. The evaporation rate of high-test gasoline is fast, but my hands were nearly frozen before I could wipe them clean. My soaked trouser legs would be all right as soon as the plane was airborne and the heater was turned on.

We could not budge, however, until we let cold air into the cabin to clear out the fumes. I thought Streich would never say it was safe to start the engine and heater.

He finally kicked the engine over and taxied the aircraft away from the refueler and onto a runway marked with flags and empty oil drums.

The propeller kicked up a cloud of snow as we jolted down the rough snow airstrip and took off.

Looking down on Little America gave me a thrill. The orange buildings stood out in stark relief against the white surface. Like a snake, the tractor trail curved to the edge of the ice shelf and over the bay ice to the ships. I had imagined a light trail on the snow would be about as difficult to distinguish as a white kitten playing on a fluffy white bedspread, and was amazed to learn how clearly visible a white track on white snow is from the air. Perhaps the visibility of the trail was due to the strong shadows cast into the ruts by the sun.

I recalled how bleak the barrier had been only two weeks before when I rode over the same area in a helicopter. Now the base looked half completed, and the snow was so completely disturbed by tracks and cargo that the site might just as well have been occupied for a year.

We made a pass over the *Arneb* for a compass and radio check, then followed the trail Bursey had left. Flags mounted on bamboo sticks were easily visible from the low altitude at which we flew, and Little America became a smaller speck in the distance as we winged in an easterly direction toward the trail party.

A high overcast obscured the sun. In spots we appeared to be flying in white-out conditions, but a few moments later we could see the trail below us again. Streich climbed to get above the overcast but could not. He let down to a lower altitude and tried to pick up the trail again. There was nothing to see but white snow.

Taking a course normal to the direction of the trail, Streich crisscrossed the area until he sighted the trail flags. We did not lose them again. At low altitude we turned when the trail turned and flew straight when it ran straight.

In two hours we sighted the party and made a ski landing alongside. Weather closed in, prohibiting a reconnaissance flight ahead.

While the gasoline tanks were rolled from the plane to a sled, one to replace fuel that had been expended by the surface vehicles and the other to be cached beside the trail for use by aircraft if an air search ever became necessary, I talked to Bursey. He was optimistic and said everything was going about as well as could be expected. I said hello to Big Ed Edwards, Charlie Wedemeyer, Ray Dube, and George Moss. The others were making camp, and I did not want to bother them.

Streich was anxious to leave before visibility got so bad he could not see the snow surface. As it was, the vehicles were already obscured when we took off.

The flight back to Little America was very much like the trip out. Visibility alternately lifted and lowered, but we soon picked up *Arneb*'s radio homing beacon and landed safely on the Little America airstrip.

Every day Jack filed a radio "situation report" to Little America. Considering the odds, his progress was better than any of us could have expected. The best time for vehicles on trail is either early or late in the season when the ice is hard. He had departed in midsummer, January 14, when the snow was softest, and had to force his vehicles over snow which could have been easily navigated a few weeks earlier or later.

We followed Bursey's reports with great interest, even after we left Little America on *Arneb* and began steaming for McMurdo Sound. He passed through a dangerous region of crevasses at Prestrud Inlet and finally attained the Rockefeller Plateau. Each day we plotted his position a few miles ahead of his last reported penetration.

The Otter plane continued to give him support, but soon the little craft was operating at almost maximum range. As often as not, Streich would park the Otter alongside the trail party's vehicles and live with the crew because the weather was too bad to take off safely.

When we arrived at McMurdo Sound, Admiral Byrd moved aboard the *Arneb* for the trip to New Zealand. The rest of the staff, including myself, joined Admiral Dufek on board *Glacier*.

Bursey's evening report showed he had encountered a heavily crevassed area at mile 380 on the trail, just over halfway to Byrd Station. Because of the closing season, Commander Whitney directed him to abandon the effort and make preparations to fly back to Little America. Lloyd Beebe, the Disney cameraman, flew out with the plane which would bring the seven-man party back in two trips.

All of us on the Admiral's staff shifted to the *Eastwind* early on February 3. Later that morning we got an emergency dispatch from Little America saying that the Otter had taken off from the trail with Big Ed, George Moss, Chuck Stevens, and Tex Gardiner of the trail party and was overdue at its base. Bursey, Dube, Wedemeyer, and Beebe had waited for the second flight.

Admiral Dufek ordered search procedure to commence immediately. Bursey was told to backtrack toward Little America while Chief Warrant Officer Vic Young proceeded at best speed with the tractors that had been intended for the fuel cache mission. It was hoped that the two surface parties, searching from either direction, would locate the airplane somewhere along the trail.

Long-range aircraft had been evacuated to New Zealand and the United States when the bay ice began deteriorating in January, so there were no qualified search planes to press into service. At McMurdo Sound two Otters were readied for search missions but encountered bad weather that forced them to abandon the flight to Little America.

Captain Cordiner aboard the *Glacier*, with an Otter on the flight deck, was sent to Little America to supervise the search. Due to the height of the barrier and the surging of the sea when *Glacier* arrived, this plane was destroyed during the unloading. Now there was only one left.

Rather than wait for the other Otter to arrive from McMurdo Sound, Captain Cordiner commenced search patterns with the helicopter that was based at Little America.

The long-range planes in New Zealand were alerted to return to McMurdo Sound as soon as the bay ice was strong enough to support them.

Bursey and Young met on the trail February 6, two hundred miles east of Little America. Their search had been fruitless. They set up camp to serve as a local search central when aircraft arrived from McMurdo Sound by ship. Lloyd Beebe had driven the Sno-cat all the way back, despite the fact that the power steering unit was inoperative.

The Admiral and I were having breakfast aboard *Eastwind* when the radio messenger brought word from the task force air squadron in Patuxent River, Maryland:

"P2V 12466 cleared for Little America via Manus, Brazil; Ascencion, Paraguay, and Río Callegos, Argentina. Pilot Torbert. Request permission to proceed."

The Admiral handed the message to me. "What do you think, Paul?"

"They have planned this flight well, knowing the distances and weather involved. Jack Torbert is one of the best. If anyone can make it, he can. I recommend you give him permission."

The Admiral nodded, and I grabbed for a message blank.

"Your message approved."

Torbert departed Patuxent River February 7. Next day we received another blow:

"P2V 12466, Pilot Torbert, crashed in clearing, Latitude 09-18 North, Longitude 62-05 West. Search and rescue under way."

I plotted the position on a chart. "That's in Venezuela, Admiral. He's down somewhere along the Orinoco River, very likely in a jungle."

An amplifying message informed the Admiral that three rescue planes were en route to the P2V, as well as Army and Air Force helicopters from the nearest base.

We loaded the remaining Otter plane aboard the *Eastwind* and steamed at best speed for Little America. *Glacier* had reported the ice shelf at Kainan Bay to be extremely high for unloading cargo as fragile as an airplane, so we searched for a low point in the barrier as we raced toward Little America.

We saw an indentation in the barrier and what appeared to be a low spot in the back end of a gorge. On investigation we learned that the barrier was not safe enough to hold the plane, so we began to turn around. In turning, wind caught the ship broadside and forced it against the edge of the ice shelf. One wing tip of the Otter was crushed by the ice.

Eastwind proceeded toward Kainan Bay. Somehow we had to get the wing tip repaired and the plane safely on the ice. Two Marine Corps sergeants, members of the air squadron, were aboard the *Eastwind* to take part in the search from Little America. It turned out that one of them was a structural expert. He made a standby wing tip and had it ready when we arrived at Kainan Bay.

We found an area of the ice shelf low enough to unload the plane, and it took off, damaged wing tip notwithstanding. Within a few hours it was flying eastward to search for the downed aircraft.

The Otter had been lost since February 3. It was now February 9. The initial search for the missing plane had been complicated by a further search for the crashed P2V Neptune in Venezuela, and all work at the bases was suffering by the emergency deployment of the ships.

"I've found every man lost under my command, Paul," the Admiral told me. "Those men will be found!"

I wished I could share his optimism. Certainly he was doing everything humanly possible to preserve this record, but how many blows can a man take? I asked myself. His hair was appreciably whiter than it had been in Washington.

The message came while I was in the radio room: "Crashed P2V sighted and party rescued by helicopter. No casualties. No serious injuries."

I grabbed the message from the radio man and rushed to the bridge.

"I told you things would turn out all right," the Admiral said. "Now we've only got one plane to search for."

We were too concerned to give the idea credence at the

time, but the dual crashes were ironic. The Neptune patrol bomber had crashed in the heart of a South American jungle, loaded to the brim with polar survival equipment. The little Otter was down on the ice, so packed with men that we doubted there was enough survival equipment to go around.

We were still rejoicing that the Neptune had been found February 10 when another message was handed to the Admiral: The lost Otter had been sighted at Latitude 77-32 South, Longitude 154-10 West. It was a made-to-order present for Admiral Dufek, who became fifty-three years old that day.

Our relief was short-lived, however. Later in the day word was received that a helicopter, dispatched to the scene of the Otter crash, had found the plane abandoned. It began tracking the men by the slight indentations their skis and man-pulled sled had made across the ice.

At times, when the men's trail was obscured by drifting snows, the helicopter pilot and observer would orbit slowly in ever widening circles until they picked up the tracks again. Finally, nearly fifty miles from the crash scene, they saw tiny black dots on the snow ahead. The helicopter landed beside the survivors, and the doctor rushed from the plane with brandy and food for the men. So great was their excitement at being rescued, they could only babble incoherently. While the doctor treated them for exposure, a radio report was made to Little America, and an Otter plane was dispatched to help bring them back to camp. They arrived safely at Little America to be greeted by steak dinners. George Moss, the trail-party navigator, had taken sights of the sun and determined that the wreck was so far from the trail that it was not likely to be found by search

five yards away, were sometimes obscured.

After determining the exact site of Byrd Station, George Moss, SVC, stands beside the marker he erected on the spot.

Seabees sweep snow from the floor of the first building constructed at Byrd Station.

Seabees build a fence sealing off the four-acre site on which the Cape Hallett IGY station will be erected. Some 6,000 Adelie penguins were relocated.

planes. Rations were scarce, so the men were walking to-ward the sea, hoping to find a seal or penguin they could kill for food.

When the survivors were returned to Little America the Seabees had a surprise for them. Showers had been completed, and each man was treated to hot water, the first they had had since January 14.

Admiral Dufek sent the *Glacier* to New Zealand for the second YOG to join the one already towed in by *Eastwind,* while *Edisto* escorted *Wyandot* to Little Amer-ica to call for the non-wintering construction men. We on the staff stayed with Admiral Dufek aboard *Eastwind.*

The bases were self-sufficient, but one important chore remained before we could call our mission completed: We had to break a channel to Hut Point and moor the YOG's for the winter night.

Eastwind bucked the heavy ice for all she was worth. In the process, she broke a propeller shaft and was rendered unfit for further icebreaking. We had to wait *Glacier's* return from New Zealand with the other YOG, and thought we had a period of rest on our hands. We were mistaken. Storms struck McMurdo Sound with 100-knot winds. The crippled *Eastwind* was blown away from her moorings and toward a lee shore. She drifted twenty miles before she could turn around. The smaller YOG, which was berthed nearby, lay low in the water and did not furnish as much "sail" area for the wind to act on. Lieutenant Dusty Blades, skipper of the YOG, reported his moorings were holding, but I truthfully do not know what we could have done if they had not. Dusty knew it too, and our conversations over voice radio belied our thoughts.

The storm lasted three days. Every four hours I called

Dusty. He was under orders to call me if any emergency arose. But what the hell, the whole thing was an emergency.

"Father Time [YOG], this is Fangtooth [task force commander]. How are you making out?"

"This is Father Time. Estimate winds at sixty knots. Moorings holding."

I didn't have the heart to tell him that we were recording 100-knot winds. Our wind speed indicator only went up to 100 knots, but it hit the stops frequently.

I have been through storms in the North Atlantic, North Pacific, South Atlantic, South Pacific, the Sea of Japan, the Bering Sea, the China Sea, and the Gulf of Alaska. I have weathered typhoons off Okinawa and Japan, but I have never experienced a storm like the one we endured for three days in McMurdo Sound.

Our position was precarious because, with a propeller missing, we did not have full control of the ship. Winds blew with howling force. Spray whipped like needles across the deck. Visibility was absolutely zero. Heavy waves appeared from nowhere and covered the *Eastwind* with cold green water that turned to ice the moment it struck. Yet the surface of the sea (what we could see of it) was whipped flat by the wind.

We had just enough power to keep our bow into the gale and maintain steerageway.

Finally the storm abated, and we headed for our mooring site. All hands were put to work with mauls, scrapers, and steam hoses in an effort to free *Eastwind* of the three hundred tons of ice that had formed over her weather decks and superstructure.

While we continued to wait for the *Glacier* to return and break the heavy ice we decided to use the YOG to make some soundings of the bay so that when *Glacier* got to McMurdo we would have an attack course planned.

Admiral Dufek, Captain Thomas, and I boarded the YOG. Dusty Blades maneuvered it along the face of the bay ice while we took depth soundings with a lead line. The Admiral took his turn at the lead like everyone else. It was cold work. The wet line froze to our gloves so badly that two casts constituted a turn. After each made his two casts, he would pass the lead over to the next person. Thus we located a safe approach to what would eventually become *Glacier* channel.

I was curious to learn the details of what had happened at McMurdo Sound while I was at Little America, so each chance I got to leave the ship, I visited Dave Canham, the officer in charge of the wintering group at McMurdo. I didn't know what had happened since the *Glacier* first arrived, except that I could see the base snuggled at the foot of Observation Hill.

"What did the large aircraft accomplish," I asked Dave, "and what caused that awful hole in the side of the *Nespelen?*"

IO ─────────────────────────────

I THOUGHT things had been tough at Little America until, after the storm, Dave Canham filled me in on the operation at McMurdo Sound. He explained the chain of events, and I realized how smoothly things had gone with us.

Glacier arrived at McMurdo to save the day when it became apparent the Wind class icebreakers could not penetrate the ice to Hut Point. Each mighty ram sent cracks racing across the hard bay ice; threatening the strip where airplanes were parked. Meantime, the plane crews were waiting until the channel could be broken and the *Nespelen* could come close enough to pump her aviation gasoline to the base.

The situation was a stalemate, Dave explained. To get the *Nespelen* close enough meant breaking ice from under the airplanes.

So Commander Gordon Ebbe, the squadron commander, told his pilots to take off from McMurdo Sound, fly north for forty miles and land alongside the tanker to refuel. Such bold strategy had never been used before, but it worked.

Marine Lieutenant Colonel Hal Kolp, the squadron's executive officer, took off January 4 for an exploratory flight into Wilkes Land. He ran into a white-out but prudently banked his R5D into clear weather and headed for his alternate destination, the South Pole, to see if he could determine the condition of the snow there for subsequent ski-landings by aircraft.

It was vital that we learn whether the snow was soft or hard so that we could choose the right weight of aircraft to land men to build a base there next year. If the snow was hard, we could send a powerful but heavy P2V Neptune. If it was only moderately hard, we would use an R4D transport. If the snow was extremely soft, we would have to use a light, single-engine Otter or else stage helicopters in relays from McMurdo Sound.

The colonel's crew dropped smoke markers to the surface from an altitude of 500 feet above the snow. The speed at which the smoke bombs disappeared below the surface led Kolp to report that the snow was soft, powdery, and of low density. He returned to McMurdo.

Two days later Lieutenant Commander Hank Jorda flew his R5D over Wilkes Land, sighting terrain that had never been seen by man. He discovered two mountain ranges. The first was about thirty miles wide with peaks seven to ten thousand feet high. The second range was sixty miles wide and also had some ten-thousand-foot peaks. Except for the two ranges of mountains, Wilkes Land was like the South Pole—just one vast, flat snow plain. When Jorda passed over the "pole of inaccessibility" (considered the most difficult point on the continent to reach by air) the surface altitude was thirteen thousand feet.

Lieutenant Commander Torbert, pilot, and Trigger Hawkes, co-pilot, flew their P2V on a more northerly course than Jorda's. While Jorda was winging over mountain ranges, Torbert flew over heavily crevassed ice. The Neptune flight spanned 2,600 miles. Starting from the most southern reaches of the Pacific Ocean, Torbert turned back only when he sighted the southern reaches of the

Indian Ocean. Visibility was so good that he saw Mount Erebus from two hundred miles away on his return to McMurdo Sound.

Lieutenant Commander Joe Entrikin took off in his P2V Neptune January 6 to fly the gap between the two westerly flights. He gave the *Wyandot* a routine position report at 10:30 P.M., but twenty minutes later the *Wyandot* began receiving SOS signals.

Entrikin reported his starboard engine was failing. His altitude was 13,000 feet, and he was a thousand miles from the *Wyandot*. Between the plane and ship stood some of the highest mountain ranges in the Antarctic.

Entrikin's fuel consumption soared as the engine skipped and coughed. At this rate, he reasoned, he would run out of fuel before he could reach the base.

His crew jettisoned everything they could move; all except forty-five days' supply of survival rations and a packet of enlisted promotion examinations. Naval administration procedures do not tolerate the irregular disposal of promotion examinations, which are kept under extremely close security procedures. In effect, Entrikin toyed with death rather than violate security, even though there was little chance that the exams would have ever been compromised through dropping.

Heaters in the plane were turned off to save fuel and the temperature fell to minus twenty-one degrees.

At McMurdo Sound planes were made ready to fly out and escort the crippled P2V or to drop emergency rations if it had to land. Should the terrain prove suitable, a P2V might even land on skis to pick up survivors.

Torbert hastily refueled from the *Nespelen* and roared into the air to escort the lame duck back to its icy airstrip.

With all spare weight jettisoned, Entrikin was able to clear the mountain tops, and he slowly made his way back home. Ten minutes before he landed, his starboard engine failed completely. He settled down with 150 gallons of gasoline, enough for only a few more minutes in the air.

On a 2,350-mile flight January 7, Colonel Kolp filled in the gaps Entrikin had missed. Once beyond the coastal mountain ranges he found only white snow plains.

Admiral Byrd made his third flight over the South Pole January 9 in an R5D flown by Commander Ebbe. Markers they dropped indicated that the snow was *hard*.

In view of the conflicting reports of the snow's density at the pole, Admiral Dufek would be hard pressed to choose the right plane for the first landing at the pole during the second year's operations.

With the sea ice at McMurdo breaking up badly, Admiral Dufek gambled. He launched the three remaining flights the same day, all in different directions. If one craft crashed there would be a search plane held in reserve. If two crashed, rescue would be very difficult and the Admiral would be a goat for gambling. If all three were forced down, rescue would take weeks.

Commander Ebbe flew into an unexplored region of Wilkes Land. No major discoveries were made. Kolp filled in another gap, learning that the maximum altitude of the polar plateau in Wilkes Land was fourteen thousand feet.

Captain Cordiner, Commander Hawkes, and Lieutenant Commander Torbert flew all the way across the Antarctic continent to the Weddell Sea and returned. They discovered a new range of mountains en route, adding credence to the theory that the Antarctic continent is actually a continent instead of a chain of islands connected by the ice cap. The 3,400-mile flight was the longest ever made in the Antarctic. Actually the risk factor was small because the same type of plane had set a world distance record some years before by flying non-stop from Perth, Australia, to Akron, Ohio. But if the plane had crashed on its extreme flight limb, rescue of its crew would have been nearly impossible.

Nine long-range flights completed, the airplanes were evacuated to New Zealand. One of the R5D's stayed in New Zealand while the other planes returned to their home base at Patuxent River, Maryland.

Then *Glacier* was free to push her nose into the ice that had been the airstrip. It broke easily and thousands of acres of ice moved north and out to the Ross Sea.

With the big slabs blown northward by the wind, *Wyandot* and *Nespelen* had to race out of their path on several occasions. *Wyandot* escaped every threat, but *Nespelen* was less fortunate.

A tremendous floe of ice bore down on the helpless tanker. Before her crew could sever the mooring lines to get the ship under way, the sharpest point of the big slab crunched through the ship's hull. Temporarily stopped by the impact, the ice pivoted in the wind, its nose mired in the *Nespelen*'s side. It worked severe damage, ripping plates apart and bending frames that held the ship together. A hundred forty thousand gallons of precious aviation gasoline spilled into the frigid water.

Once the ice completed its pivot, it floated free of the *Nespelen* and out to sea, leaving open water alongside the ship so that repair crews could patch the hull and prevent the vessel's sinking.

Meantime, construction of the base was progressing.

With a shorter distance to go, tractors dragged hundreds of tons of cargo up to Hut Point to build the base.

Wyandot was almost unloaded February 3 when the search for the missing Otter threw everything off schedule. The tank farm at McMurdo Sound was completed February 11 and *Nespelen* discharged her remaining gasoline into the tanks. *Wyandot* returned to finish unloading the same day. *Nespelen* left for New Zealand while *Wyandot* took a small amount of cargo to Little America.

With Captain Cordiner leaving the Antarctic aboard the *Wyandot* when it sailed from Little America, I became Operations Officer. As such, I issued orders in the Admiral's name.

His voice call on radio was "Fangtooth." It was not long before the name "Fangtooth Junior" was tacked on to me. The Admiral shortened it to "Junior."

We remained aboard the *Eastwind*. Time now weighed heavy on our hands as we waited for *Glacier* to show up with the second YOG.

Frequently the Admiral would say: "Junior! Break out the cards. I'm going to beat you again at gin rummy."

Each time, I would explain that the only reason he could beat me was that I considered it impolitic to beat my boss. We both liked Martinis, and it was three months since we had seen anything stronger than water. We played gin rummy for hours at a time, at a penny a point. The loser would pay off in Martinis when we returned to civilization.

Admiral Dufek also began to write a book. When he was not writing, or playing gin rummy, we would ski for exercise. The base was in its final stages, and once a day we would ski or walk from the ship to the base and hop a weasel back.

While exercising, I noted the various spots suitable for a sheltered YOG mooring. There weren't many. The best seemed to be in Winter Quarters Bay at the foot of the base site. Another was below Arrival Heights, an ever so slight indentation close to Hut Point.

Winter Quarters Bay was the obvious choice. It would be simple to break into the small bay with the *Glacier*, tie up the YOG's, and head for home—we thought.

Glacier arrived with the second YOG March 2. Pat Maher had made a fast tow from New Zealand and when he stood into McMurdo Sound with the YOG we thought he had gone berserk and was delivering an iceberg instead of a fuel barge. Spray had broken over the craft, covering it with ice.

We moved aboard the *Glacier* and sent the *Eastwind* to New Zealand, where she could enter drydock for repairs.

The ice broke easily. Soon a channel led into the small bay. Although the *Glacier* spent four days breaking through and her officers had become familiar with the shallow water, she ran aground on an uncharted shoal.

We invoked one of the oldest procedures known to seafarers—"sallying ship." The crew was massed on one side of the flight deck. On signal, they raced to the other side and stopped. Once more on signal they raced back to the other side. This shifting weight, combined with the engineers' shifting of fuel in *Glacier*'s heeling tanks, broke the ship free of the reef within an hour and a half.

Because of the shoal water, we had to settle for Arrival Heights as a mooring site for the fuel barges.

Admiral Dufek placed me in charge of mooring the YOG's.

My principal problem was to bury the little ships' anchors in a hill side some 140 feet above the water.

I brought the YOG's into Winter Quarters Bay, and they dropped their anchors on sleds placed under their bows. Tractors hauled the anchors to the top of the hill and dumped them on the frozen volcanic ash that passed for dirt. Our next problem was to bury them.

When spades and pickaxes had no effect on the frozen soil I reluctantly tried shaped explosive charges. Twelve and twenty-four pounds of TNT could blast a hole through steel. I preferred not to use the charges because concussion from the explosion might cause leaks in the nearby 100,-000-gallon aviation gasoline tanks. I could visualize the first charge rupturing a tank and letting gasoline flow down the hillside.

Over gin rummy one day the Admiral told me that if we were ever unsuccessful in any operation we would go to Tahiti and hide our heads. When I signaled the demolition man to explode the first charge near the tank I hoped it would at least be warm in Tahiti.

The tank sounded as if someone were beating it with a huge baseball bat when the TNT was exploded. But it stood intact. Another charge blew the hole a bit deeper, and subsequent ones made six holes, each about three feet deep.

A Seabee chief petty officer manned a tractor and nudged the anchors into the holes. We had no earth to fill the pits; just the fine-grained volcanic ash. Dave Canham went to the base in a weasel and brought tanks of fresh water to pour over the fill. He had to rush up the hill to prevent the water from freezing in the tanks before it could be deposited in the holes. Once the water froze on the anchors, we felt they were secure.

By March 7 we were ready to moor the YOG's. Wires were passed down to the first craft and slowly her chain was hauled up to the top of the hill and connected to the first anchor. She took a strain on the chain and the anchor pulled out of the frozen ground.

Dave Canham and I had passed the messenger to the YOG, and now we stood foolishly at the bottom of the steep hill. We looked up to see the 2,000-pound anchor teetering on the crest of the hill. If it edged a few feet more it would come sliding down the slippery slope. The chain attached to it would clear the hillside like a scythe clipping stalks of wheat.

Tahiti would not be much fun if we got there without legs!

The bos'n who was applying strain on the anchor from the YOG saw our plight and released his pressure just in time. The anchor stopped precariously close to the edge of the hill and the chief towed it back into position with a tractor.

Next day the anchors held and both YOG's were moored snugly in the lee of the hill.

Dave and I had thought it only proper that we should do the hazardous work at the bottom of the steep, icy hill. We always wore crampons and lashed ourselves together with safety lines to keep from sliding into the sea.

But after the YOG's tied up, their crews packed their bags and carried them up the hill wearing ordinary street shoes. The hill didn't look nearly so steep now that something was at the bottom besides cold water.

Admiral Dufek said farewell to the ninety-three volunteers who would winter over at McMurdo Sound, and we steamed for Little America March 9. On arrival I would receive the most challenging assignment of my life.

II

WHILE I was at McMurdo Sound, Vic Young's fuel train left Little America February 27 to cache fuel along Jack Bursey's 382-mile trail for use by the tractor trains that would drag cargo 600 miles into Antarctica's heartland to build Byrd Station at 80 South, 120 West.

Bad weather plagued the train, and after a week Vic had progressed only a hundred ten miles. Then he encountered heavy crevasses.

Bursey had crossed and recrossed the area in light vehicles without any indication that it was crevassed. However, when Vic Young's heavy D-8 tractors crunched into the same locality, the movement of the snow indicated that it was not stable. He halted his train and investigated. Four crevasses, each more than a hundred feet deep, crossed the trail, their ominous cavities disguised by snow bridges.

Following normal practice, Vic probed for the center of each bridge and placed explosive charges to blast away the lids. After the explosion, nothing was left but the gaping holes. Two tractors then began bulldozing snow into the bowels of the first crevasse. Again and again their large blades tumbled huge bites of snow into the hole.

Tractor drivers would dump one load and back off to scoop up another. One of the drivers was "Fat Max" Kiel, who had built the road to Little America. While reversing, Kiel's tractor cracked the bridge of a crevasse that had not been detected. His heavy vehicle plunged a hundred twenty-five feet into the ice crater, which came to a sharp V at the bottom. The massive bulk of the machine plummeted downward with great force and became wedged in such a way that Kiel was crushed in the cab. He died instantly.

Big Ed was lowered by rope to see if he could rescue his pal. He came up to report that any attempt would be absolutely hopeless. Kiel's body could not be recovered from its icy grave because there was no equipment capable of lifting the tractor out of the crevasse. The corpse was permanently encased within its steel coffin.

Chaplain Peter Bol was rushed from Little America by weasel to conduct the funeral services at the edge of the crevasse. The American flag was raised over the scene in one of the most poignant military funeral services ever conducted.

(Later named "Chaplain of the Year," Peter Bol was killed in an airplane crash in 1958.)

It is extremely difficult to explain the intense friendship that grows among men engaged in a dangerous assignment. The difficulty of the task, compounded by the lateness of the daylight season and the increasingly severe cold, created a major morale problem. In this instance, the reaction was increased considerably because Max Kiel had endeared himself to his shipmates long before they encountered crevasses. At any rate, the men were at the absolute breaking point when Kiel died. The mission was abandoned, and Vic Young returned to Little America the same day we arrived from McMurdo Sound, March 10.

In the *Glacier's* wardroom Young explained what had happened. He spoke without fanfare and made a gallant attempt to hide his emotions. Immediately we saw through his obviously false composure and realized that everything that had been done toward establishing the trail to Byrd

Station during Deep Freeze was in vain. The whole effort must be begun anew at the start of Deep Freeze Two.

I accompanied Admiral Dufek to Little America after we had talked to Vic Young. We were astounded at the progress the Seabees had made since we left. All buildings were completed, the radio antenna field was in operation, supplies were stowed much more neatly, and now tunnels connected all the buildings.

During the winter night snows would cover the camp. Tunnels would serve as access between one building and another. There had been no need to construct such tunnels at McMurdo Sound because that base, on land and in the path of constant winds, would be kept clear.

When we had made a tour of the camp, Commander Whitney called all his men together in the mess hall. There was an air of foreboding among them. Normally boisterous and jocular, they seemed morose as the Admiral stood before them.

Dufek made a few remarks of farewell and asked if there was anything he could do before sailing for home.

"Yes, sir," a spontaneous voice said. "Let us name something for Max Kiel!"

"By all means," the Admiral replied. "What would you want to name for him?"

"How about the airstrip?" the voice insisted. "The base is already named Little America and the bay is already called Kainan Bay."

"That's it," the Admiral agreed. "As of this minute, the strip is officially named 'Max Kiel Field, Little America Five.'"

We returned to the *Glacier* by weasel. As the ship got under way from the majestic ice shelf I waved to Herb

Whitney and his gang, pulling the toggles on the "dead-men" that held *Glacier* fast alongside.

We were on the port wing of the bridge, looking at Little America in the distance over the top of the ice shelf when the Admiral turned to me.

"Paul, we've got to get Byrd Station built *early* next year. We have committed ourselves to the Air Force for cargo drops at the South Pole. We can't increase their mission at this late date without diverting additional Globe-masters and getting additional appropriations.

"Also, we have a limited amount of gasoline.

"And Byrd Station has to be a tractor train operation with minimum air support!"

I openly agreed with the Admiral and secretly cringed at the plight of the officer he would name for the under-taking.

"Paul, that's your job next year!"

He might just as well have told me I would be the first man sent into outer space.

"I don't want any more lives lost, so make your plans carefully," he said.

"Aye, aye, sir," I gulped.

His eyes bored holes in me. We went below for coffee. "Now I'll beat you at gin rummy," he said as we stepped into his cabin.

If a gin-rummy player ever faced a handicap, I was he. The Admiral beat me out of the price of seven Martinis before dinner was served.

After dinner the Admiral asked me for a chart. He traced a route that circumnavigated the Antarctic conti-nent.

"Tell Captain Maher to follow this track. We will

investigate here and here and here." His finger pointed to blank areas on the coast line. Not one to overlook an opportunity to get a first-hand view of future base sites, even at this late date, he was going to take a look for himself.

There was no ice along our track out of the Ross Sea to slow the *Glacier* below fourteen knots. We did not encounter any of consequence until we neared the Knox Coast, and the islands that I had visited eight years before. We had called them Point Thirteen then. Now the region was named Vincennes Bay and the islands were the Windmill Islands.

High on one of them we noticed a cairn built of rocks. *Glacier* put out a boat to investigate it.

Captain Thomas, in charge of the boat party, found two notes in the cairn. The first reported an Australian party had landed, built the cairn, and deposited the note on January 19. The second note reported the Russians had visited the same spot March 9, the day we left McMurdo Sound.

Our visit was made March 18. That meant we had passed the Russian ship *Ob* sometime in the past few days. It was strange our radar had not picked her up because we undoubtedly had sailed close enough aboard.

We continued with our mission to find a base location somewhere on the Knox Coast that allowed both access to the continent and an offloading spot for cargo ships. Once we had such a site located we were to take radar photographs of the Prince Harald Coast where the Japanese planned to build a base. They had requested assistance in locating a site. Then we would investigate a possible station site at Latitude 70-39 South, Longitude 15-00 East for a proposed United States IGY station. Finally we would establish a depot in the vicinity of the Weddell Sea as a tentative site for another United States station and take oceanographic stations as opportunity permitted.

Glacier edged into a low spot on the ice shelf. A helicopter reconnaissance flight disclosed a small island that suited our needs, and a party was sent ashore to survey the route to the island, lay out the site, and sound the beach approaches. Conditions indicated it was unsafe for *Glacier* to approach nearer without more adequate soundings, and it was too late in the season to risk grounding her again.

Two hours after the boat left an unpredicted storm descended on us, and *Glacier* was blown away from her moorings. As soon as the blizzard ended, a white-out rolled in.

Glacier nudged her nose into the barrier and kept her engines running to hold her position. Her foghorn was blown regularly to signal the ship's location to the returning party.

We *hoped* they were returning. The men on the ice might be bedded down for the duration of the storm. We pondered their fate. Were they following their tracks back to the point where they had left the ship? We hoped not because we had been forced to move, and we feared that in the white-out they might walk off the edge of the barrier. There was also a good possibility that the high wind might blow them into the sea.

We kept the *Glacier*'s nose into the barrier and continued to sound the foghorn. In about two hours the boat which had landed the surveyors appeared alongside. It was covered with ice, and the deck crew had a hard time hoisting it aboard. With the wind blowing so strongly and the ship rolling heavily in the sea, we almost lost the men before we could get the craft aboard.

Still the survey party did not appear at the barrier's edge. We continued to wait and pray for seven hours. Men on deck strained for a glimpse of something besides the sea of white.

Finally there was a dot on the white landscape, then the dot became a man. The leader, we could tell, was lashed to the second, and so on. If the first man did step off the edge of the barrier others behind him could break their stride and prevent him from falling into the water.

The survey party posed an eerie sight in the white-out. They seemed to be walking on a cloud as they approached. There was no horizon to orient them in our eyes.

On they came, like ghosts. A ladder was hurriedly lowered from the *Glacier's* bow to the ice barrier, and the men climbed on board, covered with ice. They had been returning to the ship when the storm hit. They had heard the ship's whistle all along. But visibility was so bad they did not dare head back until they could see.

There were other spots that we knew were better from our survey of eight years before. Captain Ketchum could choose one of them when he brought the ships in next year. It was too late in the season to tarry, so we steamed on to the next site.

Two hours later we were in calm seas with bright skies overhead. Behind us the storm still raged. *Glacier* made her way through light pack ice to the open sea and headed west to the next destination.

Unless we were engaged in operations, time dragged. Books were dog-eared from use, and the cards were almost too thick to shuffle. Magazines were non-existent; we had

had no mail for several months.

Admiral Dufek and I continued our gin-rummy game as *Glacier* rolled in the open sea taking oceanographic soundings.

Members of Antarctic expeditions are extremely conscious of the rules of primacy. Everything is tested by the yardstick: "Is this a *first* or has somebody done it before?" We did fair to establish another *first* by playing gin rummy all the way around the world.

Glacier was extremely uncomfortable in the open sea. We could not stand, sit, or lie down without bracing for the normal roll of thirty to forty degrees. The higher in the ship, the more telling the effect of each roll. Only when we were in the ice was life worth living.

On the 17th of March we saw a radio message from the *New York Times* addressed to correspondent Bernie Kalb, who had been first into the ice and now was becoming the last to leave. The message contained the time schedule of the Russian expedition at the Knox Coast.

Russians had landed January 6 and selected their base site. January 19, they had expanded their base; January 27, disputed United States theory on Bunger Oasis; February 1, established contact with the Australians; February 2, the ship *Lena* explored Oasis (an intended Russian base site); February 7, Moscow radio said a Soviet plane had made a 1,625-mile flight and established that it was possible to set up bases in the heart of the continent; and March 10, Moscow radio reported the discovery of three islands off the Knox Coast.

"Let's discover something," Kalb urged the Admiral over coffee as he read the message.

"We have complete charts of the area they are 'discovering' things in. One island is named Frazier Island after Junior here. American planes photographed the entire area in 1946–47 during Operation Highjump. They must not have bought their charts from the U.S. Navy Hydrographic Office."

Bernie turned to me and asked:

"What does your island look like, Paul?"

"To my knowledge, I never saw it. But it was in the group we surveyed in 1948. It was reported to me that it contained the largest deposit of penguin guano anyone had seen to date."

"Well named," chuckled Bernie as he ducked the doughnut I threw.

There was a frequently told tale about how Bernie Kalb had treated Saul Pett of the Associated Press one day at McMurdo Sound. They had been out scouting for news and taking pictures when Pett fell into a crack in the ice. He sank to his shoulders and asked Bernie to help him out. According to the story, Bernie would not oblige until he had slowly maneuvered his camera into position, checked the light reading and adjusted his aperture to take Saul's picture.

Bernie, like Bill Hartigan, the NBC cameraman still with us, had grown a long beard. His was a rich black while Bill's was fiery Irish red.

One day Bernie came into the Admiral's cabin with a bird he had caught on deck. It was a skua gull, common to the Antarctic regions. The bird did not interest Bernie nearly as much as the small insect he had found in its feathers.

He asked Captain Thomas to examine the specimen under his microscope. The Captain mounted the mite on a slide and adjusted the focus. While viewing, he talked in a quiet voice.

"It is my considered opinion that this mite could only come from your beard, Bernie. What makes you think it was on the bird?"

Bernie was taken aback until he realized Thomas was pulling his leg.

We doubled with laughter.

Glacier closed Prince Harald Coast, where the Japanese IGY station was to be located. We were in relatively high latitudes and had been experiencing a phenomenon called sunset and sunrise for some days. When the task force penetrated the ice pack Christmas Eve, 1955, the sun shone twenty-four hours a day. The eternal daylight had lasted until March.

Now, we stopped about thirty miles away from our objective to await daylight. In the middle of the night the wind increased to gale force and snow reduced visibility to zero. Weather reports indicated the storm would continue for several days, so we abandoned our reconnaissance of the Prince Harald base site and reluctantly steamed on around the continent.

Glacier was ordered to proceed to Latitude 70 degrees 30 minutes South, Longitude 15 degrees East to investigate the location of a possible "gap" station to complete the Antarctic science network during the Geophysical Year. While cruising toward the site, we discovered an embayment at 69-55 South, 19-12 East. *Glacier* nosed into the barrier and put a party ashore.

We deposited an official visitation note and marked the place with the American flag. Admiral Dufek named the bay General Erskine Bay in honor of Lieutenant General Graves B. Erskine, assistant to the Secretary of Defense for Special Projects—of which Operation Deep Freeze was one.

The ice shelf at General Erskine Bay was heavily crevassed, and we stepped gingerly over the obvious chasms. Much like a child gazing at tadpoles in a ditch, I leaned down and shouted, "Anybody down there?"

This attracted some attention, and I remembered a minor ventriloquist stunt I had practiced as a boy. Without moving my lips, I said: "Hello up there!"

"Hello down there."

"Hello up there."

Admiral Dufek and Bernie Kalb walked over to me. The Admiral lay flat on his stomach beside me and said: "Who's down there?"

I winked at him, and the voice from the depths said: "Hello up there."

By now Bernie Kalb's curiosity was complete. He stretched out beside us. "Must be some sort of echo, Bernie," I said.

"Hello!"

"*Hello.*"

"Who are you?"

"*Who are you?*"

Bernie didn't know that you cannot get echoes from a crevasse.

"Who are you?" Bernie shouted.

Bernie Kalb, New York Times!" came the reply. Bernie's face whitened.

Once more we steamed eastward along the ice shelf, looking for other embayments where stations might be built. We found another small one thirty-five miles from General Erskine Bay and named it Godel Bay after Bill Godel, General Erskine's assistant. We planted another United States flag and left a note in a container.

We then set course for Atka Bay which was westward in the Weddell Sea, and *Glacier* followed the edge of the ice pack as we ground out the monotonous miles. In open seas life again became miserable aboard the round-bottomed icebreaker.

We approached the location of the proposed gap station. Admiral Dufek and I had been alternating in making reconnaissance flights, and it was my turn to look the area over.

The plane took off as *Glacier* approached the high ice shelf. The terrain was heavily crevassed. While there was a low spot that afforded unloading possibilities, the large crevasse system would restrict any movement in the direction of the continent. Consequently, this place was ruled out as a possible base site.

With some difficulty *Glacier* worked her way into Atka Bay. By now the season was extremely late, and new ice was forming on what open water we could see. We had already stayed longer in the Antarctic seas (without wintering over) than any ship in history. We bucked some heavy ice to reach Atka Bay and arrived there March 29. Once more we buried a note and planted the flag. The bay *Atka* had discovered a season earlier was indeed a suitable base site if none could be discovered to the westward.

Further search for sites would have to wait for next year. The season was too advanced to risk getting locked in the ice, and food was running extremely low on board the *Glacier*. We had followed the old custom of leaving everything we could at the manned bases. This included most of our meat supply. By the time we reached Atka Bay our nearest thing to meat rations was canned sea food.

The Admiral now ordered a course set for Montevideo, Uruguay. We resumed our gin rummy contest, and I whittled my debt down to one Martini. If I'd had a sudden run of luck I think I would have intentionally misplayed my hand to be sure the boss came out best in the long, pleasant contest.

Over the thick, dog-eared cards, I said:

"Well, Admiral, I guess we don't go to Tahiti this year!"

"No, Paul, we have had a successful season." He seemed more relaxed and at peace with the world than I had seen him for several months.

"We logged nine successful long-range flights, got two bases built, and delivered cargo for two more bases next year. The job will be bigger next year, but I feel sure we can handle it."

"Now I'm ready to go home," the Admiral said.

"We've got three days in Montevideo and three days in Rio. Do you think we should fly home from Rio?" he asked.

Did I think we should fly home from Rio?

Did I want to go to heaven?

Suddenly fatigue hit me. It had been barely three months since we entered the ice. The pace had been so fast, the frustrations and disappointments so frequent, the accomplishments so hard-won, that now I realized for the first time I had not relaxed for ninety days. Did I want to fly home from Rio? The thought of home made me feel weak inside.

For the eighth time in less than half a year *Glacier* crossed the Antarctic Circle. It was March 30. In a week we would be saying hello to South American friends; in even less time we'd be shedding our long-johns for the first time in many months.

"Yes, sir, Admiral, let's fly home from Rio!"

12

ONCE clear of the ice, *Glacier* began to behave like an athlete spoiled by his press notices. She was like a frisky mare, out to pasture after half a year of confinement. She pitched, rolled, groaned, and splashed as we left the frozen wasteland and headed for liberty in South America.

Shipboard life was more miserable than I had ever endured. When they built the *Glacier*, the builders said she was better than any previous icebreaker *in every respect*. She had proven herself completely superior at breaking ice; she had made a record tow at record speed when she pulled the YOG from Norfolk to McMurdo Sound. Now she was proving herself more miserable than any of her predecessors. Our trip to Montevideo was only six days, but, in the weather we encountered, morale rose and fell according to *Glacier*'s moods of roughness.

Her meanest, contrariest trick of all was the way she doled out her water during the storms. Showers were small to begin with, and they seemed smaller as the ship rolled fifty or sixty degrees to either side. With water faucets adjusted to obtain the right water temperature, I stepped under the shower. When the ship rolled hard to port the cold water cut off and I was scalded. Then, on the return roll, the hot water cut out and I was frozen.

Men who had worked quietly in the ice now began to assert themselves. Each, I suppose, was so eager for his first liberty that he dared not trust himself to sit quietly and pass the time. Stories were told and retold about this one who was a "work horse" and that one who was "no damn good."

Lieutenant Dick Barton, our senior helicopter pilot, told us one evening about an excursion he had been "conned" into by Fritz Goro, the *Life* magazine photographer. Fritz, like all the first-timers, couldn't wait for a chance to photograph Shackleton's hut a few miles away from Hut Point. The lift by helicopter would put him there in minutes when a boat trip might take days, depending on how much ice lay in the bay. Being a good newsman, he got his helicopter ride.

While Fritz took his pictures he methodically reached into his pocket, pulled out rocks, and scattered them about the hillside.

Asked what he was doing, Fritz told the pilot:

"My last assignment was in Australia. Before that I was in Canada. I have always picked up rocks from one place and dropped them in another.

"Just think what troubles the geologists will have next year when they find Canadian and Australian rocks in the Antarctic. It will drive them crazy!"

Between storms we rigged a volleyball net on the flight deck. The game was spirited, and it gave us exercise we needed badly; but the sport ended all too quickly when the last ball was knocked over the side.

The medicine ball proved a poor replacement for volleyball. Our stomachs were not in condition for the rough treatment we gave each other.

One evening Father Dan Linehan, seismologist from Boston College, showed slides of some seismic work he had done beneath the Vatican while searching for St. Peter's tomb. Father Dan's instruments had been very helpful during the first year of Operation Deep Freeze. He determined the thickness of the ice shelf at Little America to be between six and eight hundred feet, and he made some other important observations at various points. But it was his personality that had come to mean most to us. It was so like him to show sunny Italian scenes to men who had given several months of their lives to polar exploration.

One day out of port there was a flurry of preparations for liberty. Officers spent hours polishing braid; the laundry worked overtime preparing white uniforms for the social functions ahead; and, for once, there was no griping about the absence of meat on the menu.

While polishing my sword I thought of the many honors and ceremonies that would be observed in accordance with the Navy regulations and international courtesy. As senior staff watch officer I had to make out the staff watch list.

No matter how long a ship has been at sea, a certain percentage of the crew must remain aboard in port while others go on liberty. It took a great deal of courage, but I assigned myself the first day's duty in port.

Glacier stood into Montevideo harbor, passing almost directly over the spot where the *Graf Spee* had been scuttled by the Germans at the start of World War II.

Astern of us and rapidly coming up on our quarter was the Russian whaling fleet. The large factory ship *Slava*, accompanied by fifteen of her catcher boats, was putting on a show. The little craft maneuvered like a flotilla of minesweepers as they came up on our port beam. As each one passed, honors were exchanged.

Soon it became apparent that we were going to reach the inner harbor entrance at the same time as the Russians.

They were on our port hand and by international rules of the road we had the right of way. Did they understand the rules?

The pilot boat solved everything. *Glacier* received the first pilot and stood into the harbor as the second pilot went aboard the *Slava*. We were moored within two piers of each other.

Official calls began immediately. A car was waiting to take the Admiral on his round of visits. While he was away, I made preparations to receive the return calls of those he saw in the morning.

Soon thousands of Uruguayans lined the dock to see the Yankee ship and the strange, bearded men aboard her.

We stood stiffly at attention as the Admiral's party returned to the ship, walked briskly up the gangway, marched through the double line of side boys and saluted the colors.

Visitors were accorded side boys according to their military or diplomatic rank. The duty bos'n, piping distinguished callers aboard and ashore, got little rest. As soon as one visitor left, another appeared.

In the midst of the arrivals I was called to the telephone which had been installed on the quarterdeck. The American Embassy wanted to know when it would be convenient for the captain of the Russian whaling fleet to call on Admiral Dufek.

"Ten o'clock tomorrow morning," I replied.

Promptly at ten the next day, Admiral Alex Solyanik arrived. He was a large, jovial man of the sea, with heavy black hair and a ruddy complexion. He wore the uniform of a rear admiral with the Star of a Hero of the Soviet Union on his breast. I had been relieved of the duty by then, and so was invited for coffee with the group.

Admiral Solyanik spoke excellent English. He admired the *Glacier* and was given a thorough tour by Admiral Dufek. Over coffee in the flag cabin, the conversation centered on our work in the Antarctic and the success of the Russian whaling fleet. Many cups of coffee were drunk, and it was agreed that Admiral Dufek would return the call the next morning at nine o'clock.

Business dispensed with, I was able to buy the Admiral his Martini that afternoon.

Next morning the party gathered for Admiral Dufek's return call to the *Slava*. The Russian Admiral had brought three officers with him to the *Glacier*. On leaving, he insisted that "at least ten" accompany Admiral Dufek.

Bill Hartigan, the NBC cameraman, beat us there. He had arranged for a truck and had his sound camera going when we arrived alongside the whaling vessel.

We were taken on a tour of the factory ship. It was clean, and a practiced eye could tell it was a taut ship. The merchant seamen came to attention as the party passed and remained at attention until they were clear of any given area.

We thought it rather unusual to find women in evidence. One, we were told, had been going to sea with the whaling fleet for forty years. Her husband had died a few years back, but she still carried on. The dentist and doctor were women; clerical work was done by women, and a woman served us in the Admiral's cabin.

We had treated the Russians to coffee and conversation aboard the *Glacier*. They reciprocated with champagne, Scotch, vodka, beer, brandy, whiskey and at least two dozen sea-food delicacies. (Navy regulations forbid the consumption of alcohol aboard American warships unless prescribed for medicinal purposes.)

At nine in the morning it was a bit hard to do justice to the banquet that was spread before us, but we made an honest effort, answering toast for toast.

Finally we were invited to see a movie about the whaling fleet. Just as is often the case aboard an American ship, the reel broke in the middle of the showing. Men scurried to repair the film, but we laughed at the similarity of circumstances.

We exchanged presents and returned to the *Glacier*. The truck we sent to pick up Bill Hartigan still was not back after an hour, so we began to get concerned. Finally it drew alongside, and Hartigan carried his equipment aboard.

"What took so long, Bill?" I asked at the gangway.

"The truck driver was playing boogie-woogie on the piano in the recreation room of the *Slava*. Russians were dancing like mad and I was taking pictures. The driver was the hit of the party."

The night before we left Montevideo, Admiral Dufek was guest of honor at an American Embassy party. Then we departed for Rio.

Three days later we docked and underwent the same strict protocol, except for exchanging calls with the Russians.

Admiral Dufek and I checked into the Copacabana Hotel. On the beautiful beach in front of the hotel we took a sun bath, with Captain Thomas. After so many months in the ice it was wonderful to do nothing but stretch lazily in the warm sand and watch the South American bathing beauties doing the same thing a few yards away.

LCM's swung over the port side of the USS *Arneb* list the ship ten degrees to permit the repair party to weld a crack in the starboard waterline caused by ice pressure.

The USNS *Merrell* and USS *Atka* secured to the barrier ice in Kainan Bay to unload supplies for Little America V.

A crated Otter aircraft is unloaded in Kainan Bay for Deep Freeze II operations.

A helicopter based aboard the USS *Staten Island* flies past an iceberg while on ice reconnaissance in the Weddell Sea.

At last we saw the lovliest sight I had seen in some time—the New York sky line. Mrs. Dufek met the Admiral, and they remained in New York to keep several press, television, and radio appointments. I flew on to Washington with the group that had come to greet the Admiral.

At the staff building I ran into my old friend Charlie Browning, who had reported in while we were away. It was good to see him again after seven years. We made plans to get together after my leave, but tomorrow I would fly to Missouri to be with my family for a few weeks.

Tomorrow seemed such a long way off.

OPERATION
DEEP
FREEZE
II _____

13

BY the time my leave expired, all members of the staff were back in Washington. Now that everyone had a trip under his belt and had thus qualified as an Antarctic "expert," a different attitude prevailed in conference rooms as we planned Deep Freeze II. Officers who, lacking experience, had sat back and listened as the first phase was planned now spoke their minds with great vigor.

The major difference between Deep Freeze I and II was the magnitude of the second operation. Two bases had been completed in phase One; five would be built in the second operation.

Captain Thomas got his own task group for the Knox Coast operation; Captain Ketchum doubled as Deputy Commander of the Task Force and Commander of the Ross Sea Task Group; Captain Edwin McDonald reported as Commander of the Weddell Sea Task Group; Captain Cordiner was given command of the air squadron; and Captain Duke Calder, who had run the rear echelon during Deep Freeze One, became Operations Officer. Charlie Browning relieved me as Ship Operations Officer, and I knuckled down to my new job as Task Unit Commander for delivering the goods to Byrd Station.

The task force was greatly expanded. The Ross Sea group would include the icebreakers *Glacier, Atka,* and *Northwind,* the cargo ships *Arneb, Towle, Greenville Victory,* and *Merrell,* the tanker *Nespelen,* and the seaplane tender *Curtiss.* For the Weddell Sea operations, Captain

McDonald got the icebreaker *Staten Island* and the cargo ship *Wyandot*. A destroyer escort, the *Brough*, was assigned as weather ship for picket duty between New Zealand and the ice during the periods of flight operations. *Northwind* and *Arneb* would penetrate the Ross Sea to build Adare Station before proceeding to the Knox Coast.

For the air arm we got an eight-plane squadron of U.S. Air Force Globemasters and the Navy squadrons scheduled to fly in would be comprised of four Neptune patrol bombers, two four-engine R5D transports, and four twin-engine R4D transports with added cabin tanks to insure range enough to make the 2,400-mile flight south from New Zealand, regardless of headwinds.

Except for *Glacier, Brough,* and *Curtiss,* the ships would follow about the same time schedule as they had followed the first season. *Curtiss,* the passenger ship for scientists, would sail late. *Brough* and *Glacier* would sail in September to be on station for the flight of aircraft about October 15.

I asked for and got experienced icecap specialists from the U.S. Army Transportation Corps for the task of blazing a safe trail from Little America to the site of Byrd Station. Major Merle R. "Skip" Dawson and Major Palle Mogensen, both veterans of Arctic icecap service and both holders of Master Mariners' sailing tickets, were assigned immediately. Lieutenant Phillip Smith would report when he got back from an Arctic tour. All three proved outstanding from the beginning of our plan-making until the operation was completed.

We settled down to plan the icecap journey to Byrd Station in the heat of Washington's summer while our men in the wintering-over party in the Antarctic dug in for the winter night.

I told Skip and Palle everything I knew of Antarctic crevasses, and they filled me in on the experiences they had had in the Arctic. In this manner we were able to solve many problems before the journey began. Immediately we had to come to an understanding on the word "crevasse." I described the snow-bridged canyon Big Ed had driven across near Little America and the one that had swallowed Max Kiel's tractor. They described the narrow, deep cracks of the Arctic. We broke our Webster's dictionary. Crevasse was described as a "deep crevice or fissure, especially in a glacier." Thereafter we concluded Antarctica has *crevasses* while the Arctic has *crevices*.

I described my plan to the majors, and asked for their comments:

"There will be three task elements. The air element will be under Lieutenant Commander Bob Graham, now at Little America. He will have Otter airplanes, a helicopter, and one or more of the R4D transports that will arrive in October, to provide support for the trail party and the tractor trains. We will thoroughly reconnoiter the area from aircraft before the first vehicle leaves Little America.

"You, Skip, will command the trail party of six Army and five Navy personnel. The Navy radioman and electronic technician are now in Greenland being instructed in the use of crevasse detection equipment. A demolition man, a mechanic, and a driver will be provided from the wintering-over group at Little America. These men will complement the three sergeants who have been promised by the Army.

"The third element, the tractor train, will be commanded by Chief Warrant Officer Victor Young, also in the wintering-over party. He will have eighteen men to run the train of six tractors, each towing two twenty-ton sleds.

"You are charged with sweeping a safe trail across more than six hundred miles of unexplored territory; nearly twice the distance any heavy equipment has ever traveled in the Antarctic. We will have utmost air support at all times."

I told them to prepare their basic plans and inform me what vehicles and supplies they would need.

"How efficient is the crevasse detector?" asked Skip.

"I have heard that the version our men are getting acquainted with in Greenland is far better than the one we tried at Little America last year," I told him. The detector I referred to had proved accurate at locating crevasses, but we had not been able to install it properly on the weasel. Hence Jack Bursey did not have the advantage of a crevasse detector.

Mogensen suggested that Lieutenant Smith should also become familiar with the detector before he left Greenland. I agreed and sent a message to that effect.

We placed a great deal of hope in the crevasse detector. The Task Force and the IGY scientists had ordered two for each coastal station that would engage in over-snow traverses, so we were anxious to hear how efficient they were. Southwest Research Institute in San Antonio, Texas, had built the instruments, and would modify them to meet any requirement we expressed.

A crevasse detector works on the principle that an electronic impulse will move at a given speed through a known mass; in our case the known mass was solidly packed snow. But if the norm of the mass is changed, the impulse moves at a faster or slower rate, depending on whether the known quantity is increased or decreased in resistance. Thus we knew that if the snow was compact underfoot we would get a standard reading, while if the impulse passed through a *void* beneath the surface, the impulse would move faster and the change would be noted on a graph inside the weasel.

Rigged on booms, fore and aft of a weasel, the detector resembles an ungainly spider. Four antennae dishes ride on the snow in front while other antennae are carried on dishes behind the vehicle. The dishes prevent the booms from gouging into the snow. The weight of the booms keeps the antennae pressed to the surface.

A signal originated in the weasel goes out in three directions: ahead and to both sides. In the cabin an instrument boosts the signal to make it audible and causes a light to flash on when a crevasse is detected. All readings are recorded on a roll of paper. If the detector could be perfected it would prove invaluable to us.

Together, we searched the archives of the government for any information on Marie Byrd Land. The only thing we discovered was a chart prepared by Ray Butler after he completed a trip by dog team into western Marie Byrd Land. The perimeter of the continent was outlined, and it showed heavy crevasses where the ice shelf met the land mass buried below.

A great deal of work had gone into the chart, but it was still too inaccurate to use for heavy tractor operations in the area without further reconnaissance. We had learned the hard way that light vehicles (in the two- or three-ton class) could easily navigate a crevassed region while heavier tractors which followed would crack through the snow bridges with fatal results.

The area where Byrd Station was to be built was a large blank on all charts, just as was most of the region over which our proposed trail would be made. "Pemmican Jack" Bursey had reported other crevasses on his three-hundred-mile trip, and I plotted those on the chart that showed Butler's findings. The large blanks remaining still frightened me.

Skip and Palle worked out the details of their reconnaissance. I was repeatedly amazed at their qualifications for the job ahead. They knew to the tenth of a gallon how much fuel each vehicle would require; how thick a natural ice bridge must be to support a thirty-eight-ton tractor; what sunburn lotion worked best when reflected light from the snow began to blister a man under his chin; how to fill the largest crevasse safely by "folding" snow into the hole; what parts were likely to be expended, and how many replacements to carry; and, perhaps most important of all, how many sticks of dynamite would be needed to blast the bridges off the crevasses we could expect to encounter.

In the bachelor officers' quarters bar we became known as the "ice men" and were considered a bit balmy by the other habitués. Naturally our stories got taller and taller as the night wore on, but the after-hours sessions we held were very helpful to all of us. Both majors were considerably older than I, yet we were like children planning an outing. No problem was too small for us to talk over. One of us always had the answer or knew someone who had it. No question was left unresolved, because too many lives depended on our plans and the solutions we found.

When I consider the spadework that goes into Antarctic planning I always come down to one final thought: "Thank God for the little, ordinary *man* who will execute the plan; the one with foresight enough to improvise when an incident arises which is not covered by the plan!" No matter how many hours we spent planning or how many thousands of dollars we poured into logistics, the venture would succeed or fail depending on the resourcefulness of the men who would do the job.

We had two choices of route across the ice. One led through Prestrud Inlet, where every previous party had gone from Little America to explore the Rockefeller Mountains. The other lay to the southeast, where man had never trod.

Each previous trip through Prestrud Inlet, whether by dog team or by light vehicles, had run through a region of heavy crevasses. Max Kiel's body in one of them acted as a psychological red light in our plans.

We would explore both routes very carefully from the air, then make our own decision. The "old explorers" insisted we go via Prestrud Inlet, but we were wary.

It is easy to criticize. It is easier to give advice. It is easiest to give advice when the responsibility is not your own. Those who criticized our efforts also reserved the right to damn us if we were unsuccessful; we could expect no praise if we succeeded.

The job was ours, so would be the decisions. We would have the facts in hand, then make our plan and live with it. To hell with the old explorers!

Frequently our planning in Washington was made more pleasant by a radio report of what was happening to our wintered-in parties at Little America and McMurdo Sound. Reports from McMurdo seemed prolific at first. In late April the temperature dropped to minus thirty degrees there, and strong winds were recorded daily. One dispatch reported the finishing of a chapel, complete with church bell. That incident struck me as extremely amusing; I recalled how carefully Father John Condit had watched as we moored the YOG's—he didn't care whether they were anchored correctly or not, I now realized; he was just watching to make sure we didn't take the bells off them—they were earmarked for his chapel!

Dave Canham made frequent ice borings in Glacier channel as long as there was enough light to see. In late April the ice was twenty-one inches thick. May 9, it had grown another foot and a half. By then darkness had arrived, and we could only compute the measurements until the sun rose again in August. Two earth tremors, credited to Mount Erebus, were reported in May.

Material for the South Pole was packaged for airdrop, and the construction crews who would be landed to build Pole Station were sent on bivouacs to condition themselves for the ordeal ahead. Radiosonde* balloons rose to record altitudes as they recorded temperature and pressure of the upper air. Streets and huts were named for prominent admirals and favorite liberty haunts. There were Burke Boulevard, Radford Lane, Byrd Highway; Dufek Hall, Ye Olde Sack Inn, the Beverly Hilton, Suite Sixteen, and other titles dreamed up by men under trying circumstances.

On May 17 another Antarctic "first" was recorded. A supposedly spayed husky bitch gave birth to five puppies.

Temperatures ranged lower at Little America, and more snowfall was recorded. Tractors and sleds were being overhauled for use when we should arrive. Stores which had been dropped on the barrier were stacked nearer the

* Weather observation balloons that are equipped with a metal strip which can be tracked by radar to determine exact altitude of balloon.

dump. In July, the temperature dropped to seventy-eight below zero. But by then most of the outside work had been completed, and few men were exposed to the elements.

To occupy their minds, they watched movies, read books, and played indoor games. We could only give them moral support. Any illness or serious accident would have to be handled with the facilities present because no one could be evacuated until the planes arrived in October.

By June our plans were nearly complete. We began to order cold-weather clothing. Naturally I thought the Army issue was best, while the Army majors preferred Navy issue. We compromised by ordering full sets of each.

I wired Smitty in Greenland to learn his measurements. Back came the reply: "Hat 7¼; shirt 16-35; trousers 33 waist, 36 length; shoes 13; jacket, parka, and outside gear extra large."

His clothing was waiting for him when he arrived in June. It was a perfect fit.

Dawson's list of supplies continued to grow while I completed the basic operation plan. At the end of June I sent a digest of the plan to Herb Whitney at Little America for comment. I told him that air reconnaissance would begin about October 15 and the trail party would depart during the first week of November. I described to him what modifications would be required on the vehicles at Little America. He radioed back that the equipment would be ready.

The Army sergeants reported for duty and were ordered to the supply center in Davisville, Rhode Island, to receive supplies we had requisitioned for the trail mission. Soon they were joined by Kraut and Anderson who had returned from Greenland.

[157]

A last-minute crisis arose in August. We considered the quantity of explosives at Little America to be insufficient and ordered eight thousand pounds of special explosives and two hundred boxes of blasting caps. We directed that they be flown from the United States to the ice, but learned that the planes would not be permitted to carry such cargo. They already had twelve thousand pounds of trail party supplies to haul!

Hurriedly we made arrangements for the explosives to be loaded aboard the *Glacier*, scheduled to sail September 10. This meant she would have to penetrate the Ross Sea ice pack earlier, by several months, than a ship had ever done. Failure to get through by the end of October would stop us completely. She *had* to be there on time!

In effect the demand we placed on the *Glacier* was to be of profound significance. To deliver dynamite to Little America by the end of October meant that she would have to enter the pack in the middle of October and penetrate seven hundred miles of ice in two weeks, before the summer season arrived.

She had stayed in the Antarctic until April during Deep Freeze One; and had thus watched the birth of new sea ice. Now she would challenge it in October, before nature had a chance to disintegrate it after the winter night's freeze.

If she accomplished what we demanded she would prove that a ship of her class can enter the ice pack at any season of the year—a feat never before even considered to be possible! In case of a break in the barrier where a coastal base was constructed, this would mean that rescue of the camp population would be feasible.

14

UP to the very minute of departure we worried over forgetting to order something vital or forgetting to load something we had ordered. I am sure the pilots who took off from Rhode Island with our twelve tons of cargo did not think we had left anything behind.

At Moffett Field near San Francisco we checked each box off the plane to be sure none was misplaced.

To our distress, we learned in California that our navigational theodolites had not been loaded aboard the plane. This was like going on a camping trip without matches. I rushed to the nearest telephone to place a long-distance call.

"Have you seen anything of our theodolites?"

"What's a theodolite?"

"They are instruments we need for precise navigation. Two of them were placed in pyramid-shaped boxes marked 'Army-Navy Trail Party, Little America.'"

"Oh, so *that's* what those things are!"

"Yes, damn it! You have them there?"

"Sure, Commander, I'll put them on the next plane." The instruments arrived at Moffett Field the next morning, and we checked our gear aboard another plane bound for Honolulu, Hawaii.

After we were airborne the pilot told us he had unloaded a few of our boxes because the plane was overweight. No, he didn't know just *which* ones, but they would be along in the next airplane. We worried about these all the way to Honolulu. It turned out that three boxes had been left behind, but all of them arrived as promised.

There was another change of planes for the next long leg of the journey. Once more we assembled our baggage and checked each item as it was loaded for the flight to Canton Island and then to Nandi, Fiji. There would be no unloading at Canton or Nandi, so we were sure everything would be intact when we reached New Zealand.

Again, when airborne, were were told a "few boxes" had been removed from the plane prior to take-off. We had visions that they contained our crevasse detectors and navigational instruments.

We arrived at Christchurch in the late afternoon of October 3, 1956, and watched our supplies being unloaded from the plane and trucked to safekeeping in a warehouse. The aviators insisted that our missing boxes would be delivered without fail, so we checked into hotels for what we thought would be a five-day wait before we took off for McMurdo Sound. I reported to Admiral Dufek, who had already arrived, and told him we were ready for the ice except for the missing freight.

We met an even warmer social response than we had encountered on our previous visit to Christchurch. The very first night we attended three parties and declined invitations to others. The pace did not cease for the duration of our visit. Our five-day layover extended into two weeks. The party pace began to wear us down.

I accused Dick Whiting, our principal host, of using the two-platoon system on us.

"What is this two-platoon system?"

"One group takes us out to all hours one evening, and

another group the next evening while the first group rests. We never get any sleep!"

The Navy planes were poised for flight to the ice. Dave Canham's crew at McMurdo Sound had spent a hundred thousand man-hours preparing a smooth landing strip on the bay ice during the winter night only to have a blizzard dump eight feet of snow on the completed strip. Tractors were working around the clock to bulldoze the snow away to make a landing strip on the hard ice. Then, as soon as Canham reported the runway ready, the weather turned bad. When it cleared, there was more snow to remove from the runway. The frustration continued until October 15, the date we had been scheduled to arrive at Little America.

Finally, on that day, circumstances were right for the initial fly-in. Admiral Dufek was aboard the first Navy R5D that took off. If everything went well with the first flight, the remaining Navy planes would be launched from New Zealand the following day. The Admiral's landing was successful, and he alerted all planes for take-off the day after his arrival.

Our remaining cargo had arrived in New Zealand, and all our boxes had been loaded into the huge hull of the first Globemaster scheduled to fly to the ice. In addition to our six tons of gear, three Otter airplanes (with their wings removed) had been loaded into the same plane.

Skip and I were at a farewell party the evening of October 17 when our hostess came over to tell us she had heard a radio report saying one of the Navy planes had crashed on arrival at McMurdo, killing three and critically injuring a fourth crew member. I called the Task Force headquarters and learned that, just before the Navy planes arrived, a white-out had moved in. All craft were directed to make instrument approaches. Lieutenant Dave Carey's Neptune approached the strip by radio beacon. When he had the field in sight he shifted to visual landing rules and was banking for a turn when his wingtip raked the snow. His craft cart-wheeled, shearing off both wings as it crashed. Parts of the plane were scattered over a seven-hundred-yard strip.

"How about Captain Ray Hudman? Did he survive?" He was the only member of the crew I knew personally.

"He survived the crash but died a few hours ago," I was told.

A few days before, I had watched Hudman over Christchurch, as the squadron survival officer making a practice parachute jump. His shrouds became tangled in the tail section of the airplane, and his escape and safe landing were miraculous. Now his ticket had been punched. I thought, How ironic of the Antarctic—the survival officer being among the first casualties!

The other Navy planes, including the twin-engined R4D's that would support trail operations, had landed safely.

We received orders to take off October 20. Previously we had been informed by the Air Force that we would have to provide our own flight rations, so Skip and I made arrangements with the hotel manager for a picnic lunch for our trail party. We picked up four boxes as we paid our bills and got into the waiting taxi.

High over the South Island we opened our "lunch" and found we had roast chicken, ham, beef, veal, fresh milk, bread, cakes, cookies, fresh celery, lettuce, and tomatoes. There was enough to feed the whole company, so all passengers and crew men gathered to share our feast.

Far below, the southern tip of the island was just visible. The next land we would see would be snow-covered Cape Adare. Before stretching out on top of our boxes for some badly needed sleep, I asked the navigator to wake me when we passed Cape Adare so I could see the ice conditions of the Ross Sea. He must have been busy navigating, because I wasn't awakened until we were ordered to fasten our safety belts for the arrival at McMurdo Sound.

I grew apprehensive as the pilot circled the field three times to lose altitude for his landing. We were about to apply the acid test to Dave Canham's runway on the bay ice. Our plane grossed out at 186,000 pounds on take-off from New Zealand. Calculating how much gasoline we had expended during the 2,400-mile flight, I realized we would still be flying a ninety-ton weight onto the ice. We would touch down at a speed of about a hundred knots, so if Dave's runway was less than perfect we would come to a stop several fathoms under the water.

It was a beautiful day, with unlimited visibility. I could see the famous landmarks stretched out below us: Hut Point, where our orange camp buildings stood stark against the barren white; Mount Erebus with its vapor wisps reaching for the sky; Observation Hill, where Scott's Cross was erected; Glacier Channel, now ice-covered, as were the YOG's we had frozen in; White Island; Black Island; Mount Discovery and Moraine Glacier. To the east were the peaks of the Prince Albert Mountains.

The pilot guided the plane down in his final approach. His wheels touched, and we rode down the smooth ice runway as normally as if we were landing at LaGuardia Field. He reversed the propellers, and the mammoth plane slowed down to a speed he could control. He taxied off the strip and onto the parking mat. The plane's great nose section opened like the jaws of a clam, and I walked off to be greeted by Admiral Dufek.

I can always tell when the Admiral does not feel up to par. That day he tried to be jovial; but I knew that in the back of his mind was the memory of the P2V crash he had witnessed three days before.

The ground crew quickly unloaded the plane. Our gear was placed by the side of the runway where it would be loaded into R4D planes for the flight to Little America. As soon as our equipment was accounted for, I caught a ride on an open sled to the base.

The staff quarters consisted of a hut divided into separate compartments with a central room. A coffee pot perked on the stove. I greeted the staff members and the Air Force officers who would fly cargo to the South Pole.

The contrast of temperatures between the outside cold and the heated hut caused us to shed our outer garments as we stepped inside. We must have looked like a group of old sourdoughs, sitting around in our long underwear with our feet pointed toward the stove. Through a glass in the back door we could look out toward the bay and see planes sitting on the parkway, their orange tails and wing tips in sharp contrast with the white surroundings. Small dark specks moved about the planes. They were the men charged with readying all aircraft for the important missions ahead.

At mealtime in the mess hall we found a familiar scene. Father John Condit was playing the same boogie-woogie number on the same old beat-up piano he had played on my last visit before sailing in the *Glacier*. When he glanced up from the keyboard I noted a look of guilt in his eyes; no doubt he expected me to read the riot act because he had stolen the bells off the YOG's to use in his chapel.

I shook hands with everyone I could recognize behind a ten-month-old beard. The food was excellent. There were heaping mounds of meat, vegetables, and desserts. American sailors cannot be denied their ice cream, even in the Antarctic.

Father John came over to tell me that the fourth man had died as a result of the Neptune crash, and that memorial services for the dead would be held that afternoon in the chapel.

With the sun always above the horizon it is hard to keep track of time. We had taken off on the 20th of October and landed on the 21st. Early in the morning of the 22nd, the first Globemaster crashed. Its nose wheel gave way on landing, and the large plane skidded the full length of the runway. Three of its four propellers struck the ice, and the main support bulkheads of the plane were damaged. No one was injured.

Another Globemaster was standing by for take-off from the strip and a third was past its point of no return en route to McMurdo from New Zealand. A fourth plane had just taken off from New Zealand and was ordered back.

The immediate problem was to get the damaged craft off the runway in a hurry so the plane arriving from New Zealand and low on gasoline could land.

Hurriedly the Seabees jacked up the nose of the wreck and backed a sled under it. Then they towed the huge plane off to the parking strip just in time to clear the runway for the arriving Globemaster. Operations continued.

[165]

Plans were being made for the initial Pole landing. It had been decided that an intermediate station somewhere near the Beardmore Glacier would have to be set up to provide weather reports and to serve as a refuel stop for short-ranged planes flying to the Pole. Captain Cordiner wanted to inspect the Beardmore site before he ordered planes to land there with men and material to build a camp. He landed at three points near the Beardmore October 24 but wanted to make an additional reconnaissance the next day.

As one R4D took off for Beardmore October 25, Anderson and I departed in another for the trip to Little America. We carried mail and the crevasse detector. The other members of the trail party would follow as soon as an airplane was available.

I asked Lieutenant Commander Ed Frankiewicz, our pilot, to follow the edge of the ice shelf so I could do reconnaissance for *Glacier*'s forthcoming trip. There was about a half-mile strip of open water along the face of the shelf which stretched from the northern tip of Ross Island to Little America. If the *Glacier* got this far, she wouldn't have any trouble getting to Little America from McMurdo.

I cannot account for the ice-free strip of water along the edge of the ice shelf. The temperature had been as low as minus 78 degrees during the winter night, so it seemed reasonable that the sea would be completely frozen. I am inclined to believe that the seaward edge of the ice shelf rises and falls with the action of the tide, and that this gentle surging prevented the sea ice from gaining a foothold near the edge of the shelf.

Herb Whitney, Bob Graham, and what looked like the entire crew at Little America greeted our airplane at

Kiel Field. They were glad to see new faces, but I was not deluded into believing they had come out just to see us. They wanted their mail! They eyed our cargo, but I told them not to worry; we had not loaded any equipment into the plane until their mail had been placed aboard. The natives became very friendly.

Little America was much the same as when I had last seen it. Now the buildings were submerged in snow, and the passageway between buildings was a true tunnel. Entrance and exit could be made from several "hatches," but essentially there was one entrance—the garage.

We walked past the carpenter shop, the power house with its Diesel generators chugging away, the living quarters, and saw fire-fighting apparatus stowed every few feet within the confines of the tunnel. Herb showed me to my room, next to him in the sick bay. Seeing the innerspring mattress, the electric blanket, the bed light and personal desk, I compared my plight with that of the early explorers.

I stowed my clothing and then accompanied Herb to the galley across the tunnel for a cup of coffee. The tables there were stacked with mail. Men were reading the first letters they had received in ten months.

The postmaster handed Herb a stack. He ripped them open and began reading. Across the table from him, I was alone. I sipped my coffee in silence and watched his grow cold.

Occasional shouts broke the silence as pictures of newborn children were viewed for the first time, then passed around for all to see and praise. Cakes and cookies were circulated.

The master-at-arms announced it was time to set the tables for the noon meal. Men picked up their letters and boxes without further urging and went to their quarters to finish reading.

I walked down to the radio shack to greet my friends and to see if any messages had arrived for me. Ramsden, my old shipmate from the *Mansfield*, was on the circuit copying incoming traffic. I waved, and he nodded but I did not disturb him while he was receiving code. The chief radio man poured me a cup of coffee. He wore an extremely long beard while Ramsden was clean-shaven.

"Hello, Commander. Remember me? We were on the *Mansfield* together." Ramsden had finished with his messages.

"I knew you were here. Saw you last year, sleeping in a box. I didn't wake you because you needed your beauty sleep."

We shook hands and talked about old shipmates. In the years since we were aboard the *Mansfield* we had lost track of many mutual friends.

"Pemmican Jack" Bursey came in, as duty officer, to play the record "mess call." Soon the strains of a bugle wafted through the camp over the public address system.

George Ramsden and I laughed. We remembered "chow down" on the *Mansfield*, where there had been no bugle calls. We had had a bos'n mate named Faust who sounded the call on his boatswain's pipe, then announced in a foghorn voice: "Chow down!"

"I saw Faust in Manila two years ago," I told Ramsden. "He was on a seagoing tug that was tied up ahead of the *Shelton*."

At lunch I saw Anderson. Our gear had been brought into camp, he said, and was stowed in the electronic storeroom next to the radio shack. He planned to commence assembling the crevasse detector after lunch.

I took a place at the head table with Herb Whitney and most of his officers. Conversation was light as the heaped bowls of food and platters of steak were passed back and forth.

Charlie Wedemeyer, a first-class petty officer, was serving tables. He handed me a full platter of steaks, which disappeared as I passed it down the table. I shook hands with him, and he returned to the steam table to get more food.

Ed Ehrlich, the camp surgeon, sat at our table. He was already into his third steak.

"I didn't know you knew Charlie Wedemeyer," he said. "Boom Boom has become quite a man around camp."

"Boom Boom?"

"We were having trouble with our waste disposal. Latrine construction on the ice presents some problems Chic Sale never visualized in the States."

"How does Charlie fit into this?"

"Boom Boom solved our problem."

"What problem?"

"After a few months the accumulation of human waste in the pit beneath the seats made the place untenable. We tried everything. Various ideas were proposed. I suppose it was the only problem that ever stumped a group of Seabees," Doc Ehrlich meditated.

"They couldn't solve it?"

"Not without Boom Boom's idea."

"How did Charlie solve it?"

Doc had himself an audience, and he was playing his fish with every inch of the line.

"The alternatives were evident. Either we had to move

the building or chip out the frozen accumulation. Both solutions were impracticable.

"Boom Boom kept saying he had the answer, but nobody would listen to him. After three weeks without a solution the Commander gave him his chance."

"His chance for what?"

"We thought he was going to blow up the building. He is an explosive specialist, you know."

"Yes, I know. He's slated to go on the trail as a demolition man."

"Well, after all else failed, Boom Boom was given his chance. He got a D-8 tractor and bulldozed a pit just outside the latrine building. Then he placed TNT in the mass of waste and, with perfect control, blasted it over into the outside pit. The tractor then dug another pit and the waste was buried.

"We had to call on Boom Boom every month for reasons of sanitation.

"That's how he got the name 'Boom Boom'."

I wanted to ask other questions but refrained for two reasons. To go into deeper detail at the dining table would have been indelicate. Besides, Doc Ehrlich might just be pulling my leg.

A few days later I learned the tale was true. Charlie Wedemeyer, Seabee, mechanic, mess cook, and man-about-camp, was indeed the camp's sanitary engineer. He had solved a very real problem, even if he did accomplish his task with twelve-pound charges of TNT.

15

MAJOR DAWSON and the rest of our crew arrived at Little America in subsequent flights. The sergeants checked the last box of cargo off the plane and reported that not one piece had been lost on the eleven-thousand-mile flight from the United States.

Herb Whitney and Warrant Officer George Purinton studied Major Mogensen's plans for modifying the vehicles. "No strain, Major," they agreed. "We'll have this done in a few days."

Purinton took the plans to the garage and his Seabees began making alterations. Escape hatches were put in the roofs of the weasels, running boards made of two-by-four timbers were bolted to the sides to give easy entrance and exit, and a chart table was built into the rear of the Sno-Cat. We had radioed plans for the construction of small sleeping wanigans to be built on one-ton sleds, and they had been ready for several months. Each wanigan looked like a doghouse on its small sled, but it contained enough bunks for four men.

Nylon rope was loaded into each vehicle for lowering men into the crevasses and for use in steering the heavy vehicles through especially dangerous areas by remote control.

I called the trail crew into the library for a briefing. When I introduced Major Dawson the three Seabees of the wintering-over party who would complete our team appeared skeptical of the Army's ability to accomplish the job. Unless allayed at the outset, this skepticism could influence morale on the trail and even endanger the mission. I have always felt that the direct approach is best, so I spoke bluntly.

"We are charged with putting in Byrd Station. You know where it's supposed to be. It is a man-sized job to get that much cargo over such a long ice route. There has been some talk that we can't make it. If it is *proved* that we cannot possibly put the base at 80 South, 120 West, we will think about putting it somewhere else. But we will not accept any substitute location until we have tried damn hard to put the base where the IGY Committee wants it.

"We have made detailed plans, and we have studied everything we could get our hands on. We've got airplanes that will cover the area completely. From this air survey we will make the initial selection of the route. It's up to this party, led by Major Dawson, to prove the route safe for heavy tractors.

"I asked for *men* to be assigned. You were chosen. If you don't want to go, say so now!"

Every man looked me straight in the eye but kept silent. The men Herb Whitney had given me to round out Dawson's party included Big Ed Edwards, Tex Gardiner, and Charlie "Boom Boom" Wedemeyer, the cream of their crop. Each had been a member of the trail party last year.

"Major Dawson has had a lot of experience in Alaska," I continued. "Major Mogensen has had much experience on the Greenland Ice Cap and has done a lot of work with crevasses. So has Lieutenant Smith. The three sergeants, Fields, Coleman, and Krigsvold, are old hands on the Greenland Cap. The rest of you have been on the trail before. You know what it's like. Army or Navy, you will do the job. Now Major Dawson will tell you what he wants."

Skip gave a rundown on his plans. After my air reconnaissance, he would sweep the area by crevasse detector. On detecting a crevasse, the train would halt. The bridge would be blown off, and tractors would be called up to bulldoze snow into the crater.

Mogie briefed them on trail procedures and safety principles. Smitty explained his crevasse techniques, and Anderson outlined the principles of operating a crevasse detector.

"The most important thing I want to tell you," concluded Dawson, "is *not to nurse a beef!* If you've got a better way to do something, speak your piece. If you've got an honest gripe, bring it out in the open! There will be enough natural problems without inventing personal problems."

That evening we were invited to a party by Tex Gardiner, the "dirty bearded Texan" who had worked with Max Kiel on the road to Little America. The party was being given as a farewell to the three wintering-over men who had been assigned to the Army-Navy trail party.

Tex is blunt and honest, a sailor's sailor who doesn't have it in his nature to distinguish between officers and enlisted men. He judges every man by the way the man proves himself. If Tex doesn't like you, you know it, no matter whether you're an admiral or a boot seaman. That evening I was extremely pleased—first that we as outsiders had been invited to their beer party, secondly by what Tex told me.

"Commander," he said, "we didn't exactly like it when we heard you were in command of this here detail. We knew you from last year, and at times you were a pretty rough bas—you've been a pretty tough customer."

I agreed, thinking silently that it was most considerate of him to make this statement without full recourse to the blistering profanity for which he was famed.

"However"—he drew out the word in a Texas drawl—"you were always fair and square. When *we* worked, *you* worked. Today you laid it on the line. So did Major Dawson and the rest. We're mighty proud to be on the team because I don't think there's a Gawdamned 'Old Explorer' among us!"

Tex handed me the first beer, and the party was under way. He played the guitar, and everyone swapped stories. As the festivities wore on, Tex did a skit on why Boom Boom was called Boom Boom, omitting none of the details. It was hilarious.

Watching these Seabees at play, I realized what the word "indomitable" meant. Tex, Big Ed, and Boom Boom knew full well what lay ahead of them. Within a week they would be approaching the dread crevasses, when any step might be their last, to wage one of the most harrowing battles known to man. When the time came they would work quietly and methodically until the job was done. But tonight they were at play. Their secret, I realized, was extremely enviable. They knew how to face danger, but more important they knew how to relax. Navy Seabees have died for a number of reasons, but I will wager that few have died from ulcers.

Scheduling the departure of Skip's surface party for November 5, I began making long-range reconnaissance flights November 2. At least one of the Army officers accompanied me on each flight. We flew over each area three times—in the morning, at noon, and in the late afternoon.

Light and shadows play strange tricks in the Antarctic, so we had to scan the surface under each condition of light.

Areas that appeared safe in the morning often revealed ugly crevasses in the afternoon. On the first pass the sun might be at such an angle that it filled in the depressions; but in the afternoon, with the sun on the opposite side of the snow mound, the shadows gave away the presence of crevasses. I flew every hour the weather permitted. When the plane was grounded or when the crew rested between flights, I plotted my findings on a chart in Herb Whitney's office.

Preparations for the Pole landing were being made at McMurdo and so many times I had to wait my turn for an airplane to be used on trail reconnaissance. One of the R4D's had been damaged when it made a rough landing at the Beardmore Glacier. The crippled wing, seen through a window as we made flight after flight, did not tend to create peace of mind for the plane's occupants, but the damaged craft was better than nothing. Time was running out, so I was happy to get any help from the air squadron. Dawson had to start on the trail soon if Byrd Station was to be built on schedule.

The crevasse detector had been tested satisfactorily, and all modifications had been completed on the vehicles by November 4. But all planes had been recalled to McMurdo Sound, and I postponed Dawson's departure. I felt that one more flight was necessary to locate the best access to the plateau.

I had already decided on a route to the southward of Prestrud Inlet. The trail I chose had only one visible area of crevasses, about five miles wide, but I felt it absolutely necessary to make one more flight. The exact width of the belt would have to be checked by the crevasse detector.

On the 30th of October I had sent Captain Cordiner this message:

"Visual air reconnaissance imperative prior to departure of surface trail party. Further delay reduces total time necessary to establish Byrd Station. Request permission to retain broken-wing R4D Little America after next trip."

Cordiner had obliged, and in the broken-wing plane we had completed all but one leg of the most urgent part of our reconnaissance—the ramp area where the ice shelf meets the mainland of the continent. I had what looked like a good approach but I wanted to check and recheck to make sure it was actually the best. Then the plane was recalled to McMurdo Sound.

On November 3 I sent another plea:

"Imperative R4D return Little America soonest to allow one more reconnaissance flight prior departure of trail surface element. Have determined what I believe to be a satisfactory trail to 79-43 South, 152-22 West. Have eliminated other approaches. Next flight will determine route to plateau from above position. After one more flight Otter aircraft support will suffice for about two weeks. If Otter planes not ready, request R4D support until Otters ready."

The icebreaker *Glacier* completed the near-impossible by plowing through some of the heaviest pack ice ever encountered by a ship and arriving in the Ross Sea October 31. In the seven-hundred-mile pack she rarely found any leads. Ten-tenths ice coverage was the rule instead of the exception. Some of the floes were as thick as thirty feet, but the proud, powerful ship bulled her way southward. As soon as she dropped off some men at McMurdo, she steamed for Little America.

Eight ships of Task Force 43 in McMurdo Sound with Mt. Erebus in the distance.

The wreck of a helicopter that crashed on the flight deck of the USS *Staten Island*

The Ross Ice Shelf is blasted to remove loose ice.

The USS *Atka*, her bow loaded with ice, rams the barrier in Kainan
Bay to make a safe mooring.

Skip and I rejoiced at *Glacier's* achievement and our own good fortune, for she was bringing four tons of high explosives so vital to our success when it came time to battle the crevasses.

Walter Sullivan of the *New York Times* was at McMurdo Sound. On November 3 he wired: "From Walter Sullivan *New York Times*. For Frazier and Dawson. Would like much accompany trail party on initial leg returning via first Otter flight. Could reach Little America if this acceptable. Please advise."

After talking it over with Skip I wired Sullivan that sleeping space and food were limited. We anticipated the trail party's departure before *Glacier's* arrival, but we would try to comply with his request when he arrived. I told him to bring his own sleeping bag and to carry his own food from Little America.

Sullivan's reply was prompt: "Due crowding aboard aircraft, expect to arrive early November 6 aboard *Glacier*."

The reconnaissance plane had not arrived by noon November 6, so I told Skip to get under way. I would fly the remaining flight before he reached the crevassed area and radio my findings to him.

Glacier arrived four hours after the trail party departed. We unloaded the explosives by helicopter. They would be held in reserve at Little America, to be flown to the trail party as they were needed.

Disney cameraman Lloyd Beebe, who had wintered over at Little America, left with the trail party. I told him that Sullivan wanted to join the group, and he volunteered to return on the first inbound aircraft after he got the pictures he wanted.

With Skip on the trail, I grew impatient for an aircraft. I knew he would encounter a belt of crevasses about a hundred eighty miles from Little America, but I was most anxious to survey the remainder of the six-hundred-miles-plus route; but all I could do was wait, for I did not know why the planes were tied up at McMurdo Sound. I was very happy to receive Admiral Dufek's message:

"For Commander Frazier. Skymasters have not been able to fly since arriving here. If you need another R4D or anything else, please let me know. Dufek."

Lieutenant Harvey Speed arrived in the broken-wing R4D, and that was all I needed. My reconnaissance continued. The chart was full of valuable information now. Blank areas became filled in.

Each time I flew out on a reconnaissance mission I tried to stop alongside the trail party and exchange information with Dawson and Mogensen. In that manner I could tell them the results of my air reconnaissance. The trail party was approaching the crevassed area, so I thought it best to place an Otter plane at Skip's disposal for short-range reconnaissance while I continued my long-range missions.

By November 9 I was able to tell Dawson what appeared the best route to the plateau. I pointed out an area of possible crevasses directly in his path and ordered him to wait until the Otter arrived. While waiting, Skip sent an advance party to inspect the suspicious area I had warned him about. He reported that the crevasse was small, and that it would not offer serious resistance.

Lieutenant Wesley Seay joined the trail party with an Otter plane November 12. Skip was stopped at mile 171 from Little America. For the next three days short-range flights were made in the heart of the crevassed region that lay in the path of advance to the plateau.

Skip radioed me November 14 that he had finished the short-range reconnaissance to mile 180 with the Otter. He had located five small cracks across the trail and was about to examine the ramp area.

I flew out to the trail party November 15 to see operations at first hand. The flight was simple; just a matter of following the tracks made by Skip's heavy sled runners. Fuel drums sitting on snow mounds every twenty miles verified our distance. The same drums would prove invaluable aids to airplanes during white-outs because they would serve as radar markers.

Lieutenant Harvey Speed, my pilot, landed on the snow. Skip, Mogie, and I climbed into the back of the Sno-Cat and spread our charts on the table. Skip traced the area he had inspected.

"We have completed reconnaissance in this area," he pointed out. "We think a possible trail to the plateau can be established here." He tapped the chart. "It will involve helicopter reconnaissance flights for about three days. This route we have recommended violates every sound technique developed for heavy tractor train movement. We will be going parallel to the crevasses, rather than approaching them at right angles, but I believe we can reach the plateau in about two weeks. All other approaches are more heavily crevassed than this one, you say, and I'd like to return to mile 160 and come into the area at this position." He pointed again to the revised trail he proposed.

Sooner or later, we realized, we would have to tackle the crevasses. Skip's recommended route looked much less dangerous than anything either of us had seen from the air, so I concurred. To continue on the present course would have been hopeless because the area ahead was crevassed for miles. Skip's train was parked on the brink of the dangerous fissures we had plotted from our reconnaissance. This was the best area of any to make the bid to the plateau. It was advisable, however, to backtrack and re-approach to a more advantageous position, even though it would mean several days wasted.

Skip removed the trail flags he had planted as his party returned to mile 160. Then the new course was set, and the party got under way.

Reconnaissance, parry-and-thrust tactics, and speculation were behind. The battle was imminent when Skip reached mile 180 on the new trail. Nature held the edge, but still we had confidence that victory would be ours.

Skip radioed November 20 that he had reached crevasses at mile 183. His future movement would depend on close air reconnaissance, work, and sweat.

I sent out the aircraft to carry fuel to resupply the tractors. The planes pulled double duty by escorting Marine Lieutenant Pete Kenney in his helicopter. I told Kenney to stay with Dawson until he was no longer needed, thinking I would see him back at Little America within two or three days. Actually, when he returned he had grown a fairly full beard and had logged ninety-seven flights in the region which was to become "Crevasse Junction."

When the Otter planes returned to Little America, Lieutenant Seay brought a note from Major Dawson. I cringed when he handed it to me because I knew it contained news of such import as to warrant absolute privacy; otherwise the message would have been sent by radio. I opened the note to read:

"Commander Frazier:

"We camped at Mile 180 last night and moved up here (mile 184) this morning. The crevasse detector, the Sno-Cat with four sleds, one D-8 with two twenty-ton sleds made mile 184.

"The second D-8, towing one wanigan and one twenty-ton sled, observed a three-foot crack and stopped short of mile 184.

"After careful foot reconnaissance we found six cracks from six inches to three feet.

"*The crevasse detector did not register anything.*

"Recommend you visit the train for a conference.

"Dawson"

I flew out immediately, and Wes landed the Otter alongside Skip's vehicles. Skip showed me the crevasse that had stopped the second D-8. It had not only stopped the D-8, I learned; the rear sled runner of the wanigan had broken the snow bridge and had dropped in the hole. Luckily, it was a small crevasse; but it had shaken the men's confidence in the detector.

By the time I arrived, morale was high. The men were laughing about Sergeant Coleman falling into the crevasse when he jumped from the sinking wanigan. He had sunk up to his armpits, but now he could enjoy the humor as well as the others.

I inspected the crevasse. It appeared to be the tail end of a larger one running from the north. Skip's prediction had been right—they would have to run parallel to the cracks from this point to the plateau.

Skip and I talked to Andy about the detector.

"Commander, I swept the area and got no signal," Andy said, apologetically. "After the wanigan broke through I drove the detector back and still didn't get any indication of a fissure. The D-8 pulled the wanigan out of the hole and I ran the detector back and forth over the area.

"The length [fore and aft] system didn't give any signal, but the width system did. I've checked everything, but I just don't get a signal!"

"What do you think about calibrating the detector again, running over the crevasse after each adjustment until you do get a signal?"

"Recalibration might do it. The density of the snow might have changed. I'll give it a try right away." It appeared to me that Anderson felt personally responsible for getting the party safely to the plateau. He seemed eager for a chance to prove his detector could be fixed, and he was especially appreciative that he would get a chance to try to make it work. Skip and I got out of his way as he began to make adjustments.

For safety reasons, as well as for morale, the detector had to be made operable. Andy knew more about it now than anyone—including the manufacturer, who was nearly half an earth away from us. Skip and I had confidence that Andy would find the trouble. He did.

The November 23 situation report looked good.

"Two-mile safe trail in crevasse area. Light vehicle and foot reconnaissance to three and eight tenths miles. Crevasse detector giving good results after calibration."

During the time Andy was calibrating the detector, Pete Kenney had been flying the helicopter over the area. Lieutenant Smith and Sergeant Fields took turns hanging out of the cabin door to direct the flight as they marked the safest route through the maze of crevasses.

Kenney would be told to hover over a given spot while one of the trail experts leaned out to plant a flag. Soon there were flags through the entire crevasse system, marking a path which would be followed by men on skis, then by the weasel which shoved the detector.

The three miles of crevasses we had seen from the air developed into a seven-mile area of deep fissures. Still, it was the best approach to the plateau.

As Smith and Fields continued marking crevasses, other members of the party commenced blasting along the route laid out by trail flags. When the bridges were blown off the crevasses, Skip decided whether it would be wiser to fill or by-pass the individual holes. His yardstick was that if a sound path thirty feet wide could be navigated between open holes the holes need not be filled. As a result, the trail wound like the trail of a snake.

The situation report filed November 24 read: "Light vehicle reconnaissance four and three-tenths miles to plateau. Safe trail two and eight-tenths miles."

The battle continued. Each time a crevasse was blown open, Smitty, Mogensen, or Anderson would lower himself into the bowels of the fissure to determine its direction and to test the thickness of the bridge which had not been removed. If the bridge was thirty or more feet thick, it was safe to cross. If the direction twisted away from the line of advance it naturally did not warrant further concern.

While making such observations, Smitty learned that some of the crevasses' floors were lower than sea level. At first this seems preposterous; but when you consider that the Ross Ice Shelf is over water, and further, that when you float an ice cube in a glass of water there is more of

[183]

the ice under the water than there is above the surface, the situation becomes credible. The crevasses in the ice shelf were like cavities in a tooth. While the whole tooth extends below the gum-line, the cavity often ends short of the bottom of the tooth, although it may be beneath the gum.

On November 26, Skip reported: "Estimate one and one-half miles from plateau. Safe trail to mile 186.1, or three miles from camp. Request some form of medication for sun and wind burn."

The technique was paying off. Skip and his men were slowly making their way through the crevasse system, and their only worry was sunburn.

I took out a carton of Noxzema. The men's faces, especially around their mouths and under their chins, were cracked from the wind and sun. Each man grabbed a jar as a starving man grabs bread and began spreading the cream over his burning face and neck.

On November 27 the party reached mile 186.7.

Next day I learned that Lieutenant Speed was returning to Little America with an R4D for my remaining long-range reconnaissance. I had the route plotted to within two hundred miles of Byrd Station site, but needed a few more flights to finish the job. It was also getting near the time when considerable fuel would be needed by the trail vehicles, so the message was most opportune.

Wes Seay had been flying the Otter out to the trail party daily from Little America when weather permitted, with explosives, mail, and clean laundry, and had amassed a considerable fuel cache at the camp site; but the Otter was so small that it would have taken excessive flights to deliver enough fuel.

My elation over Speed's return was short-lived. Skip reported November 28: "Safe trail to mile 187.5, or 4.5 miles from camp. Revised estimate of distance to plateau three miles. Explosives on hand sufficient only until midnight tomorrow."

That was indeed a problem. The trail party had been using 800 pounds per mile in the crevasse area, and the supply at Little America was almost exhausted. The nearest supply point was New Zealand.

I asked Don Kent, the task force supply officer in New Zealand, to get me some explosives immediately. Whatever he could get would have to be flown in.

The thought of having reached the very threshold of the plateau only to become stymied by lack of explosives was disheartening.

Dawson asked for 1,000 pounds of explosives November 29. I sent Wes out with every stick we had at Little America. The situation at Crevasse Junction was so critical that the normally jocular Seabees at Little America did not even crack jokes at the fact that they could no longer blast the waste from under the latrine.

Skip radioed: "Safe trail to mile 188.7, or 5.6 miles from camp. Approximately two miles to plateau. Request ointment for irritated eyes."

Every man in Skip's party realized the seriousness of working without strong sun glasses. They had faithfully worn dark glasses while they battled the ice, but wind had burned their eyelids to the point that the pain was more severe than snow blindness. Doc Ehrlich mixed a solution, and Wes flew it out with the last of our explosives.

What appeared to be the final disappointment came November 30. Skip wired: "Encountered two crevasse

[185]

systems crossing trail at mile 188.6 and mile 190.3 which must be blasted and filled. No mileage today. Estimated time to complete blasting and filling is dependent on availability of explosives, which will be exhausted by midnight tomorrow."

Despite our best efforts at reconnaissance, Skip had painstakingly blasted and squirmed and dodged his way into the bottom of a natural V of crevasses.

I had no more explosives to send out. I had wired McMurdo Sound days before, and they had none. Had I made the unforgivable mistake of outrunning my logistics?

Skip's report December 1 gave me renewed hope: "Trail tested to mile 189.2, or 6.1 miles from camp. One crevasse system blasted, filled, and crossed. Fill required 105,000 cubic yards of snow! Contemplate one heavy sled test movement toward plateau tomorrow."

I crossed my fingers. Skip had reported *two* crevasse systems in his path; yet he reported filling only *one!* I prayed that he would have enough explosives to blast the remaining obstacle in his path.

On a reconnaissance flight with Speed, I flew over Crevasse Junction. I could see the trail snaking its way through the crevasse systems. Black residue from the explosives stained the pure, glistening white snow on both sides of the trail. For some reason, the sullied ice reminded me of a trollop who had slept with her make-up on.

Barrels and trail flags marked the route, showing how closely the trail paralleled gaping, deep-blue holes. I was filled with admiration for the guts Skip and his men had displayed. Without doubt, some of the "old explorers" I knew would have abandoned the task long ago; but as we flew over the crevasses it seemed that Skip was only a few yards from the empty fuel drum which had been flown out by helicopter to mark the edge of the plateau.

Skip's situation report December 2 confirmed what I had seen on my return flight: "One D-8 tractor penetrated trail to foot of plateau. Further test of trail with tractor and cargo sled tomorrow." Without being told, I knew that Skip had exercised his customary good judgment in getting that heavy vehicle to the plateau. He had "reined" it over the trail, attaching ropes to the gears so that the thirty-eight-ton monster could be manipulated by men walking thirty feet to either side.

Don Kent responded to my plea for additional explosives: "*Glacier* and *Atka* unable provide suitable cold-weather explosives. New Zealand Army can supply up to ten tons of TNT slabs weighing four and one-quarter pounds each with primers. Supply of number six instantaneous electric blasting caps can be obtained commercially. Advise soonest whether desirable, also minimum total required, including number blasting caps and primer for air delivery to McMurdo."

Good old Don Kent! He knew that when I asked for something I really needed it. He was turning the area upside down to get my explosives.

December 3 was the happiest day of my life. Skip's situation report said: "Two twenty-ton sleds now on plateau. Remaining equipment will follow tomorrow. Trail across crevasse area now ready for heavy sled movement. However, continuous trail maintenance will be required. Capacity of trail cannot exceed one tractor and one sled on each movement. Traffic will continue to open fissures along and across trail roadbed. Twenty-five boxes of explosives cached at turning cairn, mile 183.1, for use in crevasse area."

We had made out all right. We had plenty of explosives on hand now because air reconnaissance had indicated there were no more crevasse areas the party had to cross. All other fissures along the way could be skirted. I wired Don Kent that four tons of TNT slabs and eight hundred caps shipped via the *Glacier* would be sufficient to maintain the trail.

Vic Young and his tractor train stood ready to go. For the past two weeks he had been asking me: "When?" Today I could say: "Now!"

Admiral Dufek had flown to Little America from McMurdo Sound while Skip was having his worst session with the crevasses. Greatly relieved that the plateau had been attained, he ordered a send-off for Vic Young's tractor train that Bill Hartigan, the NBC cameraman, said was "the biggest show I've seen since Panmunjom!"

16

ON many occasions I have had reason to consider Admiral Dufek one of the Navy's greatest natural leaders of men. Perhaps his most unusual trait is an uncanny ability to sense the moods of his subordinates in a time of particular stress, and then to do something to improve their outlook.

While Dawson's party was battling nearly hopeless odds at "Crevasse Junction," morale became very low at Little America. Sitting with the men in the mess hall, swapping stories with them, and studying their personalities all the while, the Admiral decided it was time to act.

Recalling his promise during Deep Freeze I to name Kiel Field for tractor driver Max Kiel, the Admiral announced that the field would be formally dedicated immediately. The very ceremony, he realized, would serve to divert the men's attention from the plight of their shipmates, and it would give him a chance to reassure one and all.

Promptly at eight A.M., seventy-three men crawled out of the camp that had become snowed under during the winter night. Fifty yards away, they looked identical in bright yellow Byrd-cloth parkas and trousers and knee-length rubber boots that contrasted sharply with the dazzling whiteness of the Ross Ice Shelf. Unless you knew who was short and who was tall, who had a black beard and who had a red one, or perhaps the ones who had no beard at all, you could not tell one man from another at that distance.

This would be the first time the whole camp population had stood together in a group formation since they left the United States fourteen months earlier to build and man Little America V.

The men were strangely quiet for Navy Seabees—noted for their ability to complain one moment and to be light-hearted the next. The morning's business, however, was far too serious for griping, they reasoned, and horsing around would not be in keeping with the dignity of the occasion. They were gathering to pay honor to "Fat Max" Kiel.

They filed silently from camp to the waiting sled platform, which would be towed by tractor to Kiel Field, two miles across the snow. The trip took nearly an hour.

From the operations tower at the austere airfield I watched a burly chief petty officer form the men in ranks: "Cover off, you knuckleheads. Want to catch cold milling around out here all day?"

Exhaust from the tractor engine and from the air station ventilator pipe condensed in the frigid atmosphere. The driver nosed his vehicle into the snow bank that marked the edge of the runway, and killed his engine.

Herb Whitney, the base commander, and I walked to where the men stood in formation.

Directly in front of the formation, Chief Petty Officer Earl Moore, a two-hundred-forty-pounder with the blackest and fullest beard I have ever seen, held the four corners of a sheet of parachute cloth draped over a crude wooden cross. Air trapped inside caused it to billow out like a balloon, and it looked as if it would pull the huge Seabee off his feet.

Admiral Dufek had followed Herb and me and now faced the men.

"We have come to pay homage to Max Kiel," he said.

"When I heard your spontaneous desire to name this field for Max Kiel last March I knew Task Force 43 had lost a valuable man.

"But when Max Kiel plunged to his death in a crevasse at Prestrud Inlet, we learned a lesson.

"We learned it would not be possible to send a heavy tractor train through that region with materials to build a base in Marie Byrd Land."

The men listened intently to each word. Max had been a very good friend and shipmate as he drove tractor loads of equipment from the ships to the base site last season. On the trail he had been a most valuable companion when nerves wore thin in the crevasse region.

"We are taking a better route this year, and we are using special safety precautions to protect the lives of the eleven men in the trail party and the nineteen men who will take the tractor train to Byrd Station," the Admiral continued.

Then he directed Chief Moore to unveil the cross that bore a plaque to Max Kiel.

Maybe it was the cold weather, maybe it was the occasion, but it was so quiet that every man in the formation could hear the nylon crackle as it was pulled off the mute cross. The silence was more profound than any explosion I have ever heard.

One Seabee in the formation was heavily burdened with clothes and must have been uncomfortably warm. As Chief Moore pulled the parachute clear of the cross the man pulled his clothing tighter around his neck and muttered, "Gawd damn, it's cold out here!"

Tears were not uncommon in the beards. Max Kiel

was a good man, but Max Kiel was dead. At least the bleak, cold, crude airstrip had a name.

It was only a ski-strip, really. Blades from the large tractors had smoothed out the ice hummocks, and heavy rollers had packed the snow into a frozen concrete-hard surface. The radar antenna rotated, sending out electronic impulses, but it received in return only the signals that bounced back from building tops at Little America and the faint outlines of the empty black fuel drums that marked the limits of the runway.

No planes were in the air. The few assigned aircraft sat in a cold, orange-colored line waiting for their pilots and crew members.

Planes had operated from the strip since the first sunrise, a few months ago. I had landed here a few weeks earlier. From this airstrip the twin-engined Skytrain that had brought me and my men roared off and ranged over the vast ice shelf eastward and southward into the unknown reaches of the six-million-square-mile continent groping for a safe route to Marie Byrd Land.

I wondered whether Kiel felt honored by this ceremony in his memory.

Many men have died in the name of religion; many for political beliefs or idealistic social orders; and many for science. Max fell in the latter category, though I doubt he realized it. He was a sailor from Eugene, Oregon, doing his job as one of Dufek's Volunteers, and I doubt that he ever thought about death; certainly not about dying a martyr's death for science.

But I felt Max's death deeply. I didn't feel responsible for it, mind you, because of being Assistant Chief of Staff for Ship Operations at the time. I certainly was concerned over the crevasse that claimed Max Kiel, however, because eleven men under my direct command were at the very moment in a region of similar crevasses blazing a safe trail for heavy tractor loads. Nineteen other men under my command would drive heavily laden tractors over that trail when I gave the signal; and a score of aviators under my command were risking their lives by flying support to the advance trail party, and would take further risks while supporting the tractor train before Byrd Station was completed. I looked at Max Kiel's cross and wished I was still Ship Operations Officer.

Death comes easily in the Antarctic. Max was the second of Dufek's Volunteers to perish during Operation Deep Freeze. His friend, Richard Williams, had gone through a crack in the bay ice with his tractor a month before Kiel died. This year, just before I arrived from New Zealand, four more had died in an airplane crash at Mc-Murdo Sound.

I thought of Kiel, Williams, the aviators, and all the others who had been claimed by the Antarctic, and I paused to take stock of my present situation.

I held the lives of some fifty men directly in my hands during the project ahead. One misstep on the trail, one drowsing tractor driver, one miscue by a pilot, or one misplaced parachute drop of an airplane load of fuel drums, and I would become responsible for one or more new crosses erected somewhere in the barren Antarctic. What I didn't know at the time was that, once Byrd Station was completed, I would face an even more hazardous job.

How in the hell, I asked myself, did you ever get into such a predicament, you who profess to be a destroyer sailor?

Admiral Dufek had given me an assignment, and I intended to carry it out to the best of my ability. This was my third hitch in the Antarctic, and my experience was greater than that of many present; but I still felt my human, personal limitations. A man had to be one of Dufek's Volunteers and had to possess a fair share of Dufek luck in order to pull off the job that lay ahead of me. A year earlier there had been 1,800 of Dufek's Volunteers. This year there were 3,500. To a man, I believe, we'd have gone to hell for George Dufek the "old man," George Dufek the Admiral, but definitely *not* George Dufek the *explorer* —a title the silver-headed, ruddy-faced, man-o'-war's-man never assumed.

17

WHILE Skip's advance-party vehicles were being refueled at the edge of the Rockefeller Plateau, final preparations were made at Little America for the departure of Victor Young's tractor train December 5.

We were justly proud of Skip's achievement in blazing a trail through the crevasses and onto the Plateau but now the acid test would be applied to it. Lined up and loaded, Young's train weighed 1,200,000 pounds; each of the six D-8 tractors weighing thirty-eight tons, pulling a double-sled load. The empty sleds weighed eleven tons and carried a twenty-ton payload. Within days we would know whether Skip's trail was absolutely safe.

What appeared to be the entire Antarctic press corps was at Little America for Young's departure. There were television cameramen, newspaper and magazine writers, and Disney's cameraman Lloyd Beebe.

The tractors stood in a line with their engines running while Young's crew of nineteen faced Admiral Dufek for final instructions. When he had wished them Godspeed the men raced to their vehicles and lumbered away from Little America at their maximum speed of three miles per hour. One cameraman, trampled by the rushing drivers, said he thought he had been charged by the Notre Dame football team. The six huge tractors' engines running in unison sounded louder than automobiles engaged in the Indianapolis five-hundred-mile race.

Young patrolled up and down in a weasel. In that

manner he could spot any discrepancy and flash a signal for the long column to halt until repairs could be made.

When the train left Little America the tractor towing the cooking and sleeping wanigans was fourth in a column of six rigs. Before the first day ended, it had been moved up to the head of the column because the deep ruts made by the tractors and sleds ahead caused the wanigans to pitch and roll so badly that the cook became seasick.

Young would never admit it, but I knew he planned to race Dawson to Byrd Station. Dawson had a hundred-ninety-mile lead, and the odds were in his favor; but Young had an important advantage: two sets of drivers to Dawson's one. Dawson's plan was predicated on a schedule of twelve hours driving and twelve hours rest. Young, the aggressor, would drive twenty-two hours a day, changing shifts at 6 A.M. and 6 P.M. when the men ate their main meals and refueled their machines.

I have never seen a more determined group than the nineteen men who made up Young's train. Many of his drivers had been present when Max Kiel was killed. They knew the absolute despair that accompanies failure, and each man seemed resolved to do such a good job that the first year's failure would be wiped from the slate.

On December 7 Dawson reported that the advance party was at mile 280. There was no report from Young on the progress of the tractor train; but I learned later that his reason for not reporting was that he would not take time to stop long enough for his radio operator to set up his antenna. I was not concerned at his silence because I knew that if he was in trouble he would let me know.

Skip sent me a priority message December 8, saying

he had crossed last year's trail at mile 313. The intersection point was more than twenty miles out of position according to Mogensen's navigation. With that much error, Skip was concerned that perhaps his present course would take him into the crevasse belt that had stopped the previous party. He requested immediate air reconnaissance, informing me that the snow conditions where he was were satisfactory for aircraft landing.

I was positive that my plot of the crevasses was accurate, and I had full confidence in Mogensen's navigation. I knew that the old trail ended in a crevasse area, and that the region was well south of the planned trail we were following. But I summoned Speed and immediately made ready to reconnoiter ahead of Dawson.

We landed alongside, and I went into a conference with Skip and Mogensen. I asked which of them wanted to accompany me on the reconnaissance, and Dawson sent Mogensen and Smith. I bet them a Martini in Washington that we would find things just as I had plotted them many flights ago.

We climbed into the airplane and fastened our safety belts. Speed revved his engines and applied full power. The R4D bounced along the trail for five miles but would not take to the air. We taxied back to Dawson's vehicles and made a second attempt. Once more we failed to take off. Speed returned to the tractors and pumped some fuel into the storage tanks, assuming the plane was too heavily loaded for take-off.

Once more he gunned the engine, and we bounced from snow ridge to snow ridge. Finally we did not return from a bounce, and the plane was airborne. We circled the tractors for the navigator to get his fix, then flew our planned course.

Below us the snow appeared solid and safe. Only on the southern horizon, twenty miles away, could we see the telltale lines of the crevasses with the old trail running into their very heart. Our planned route would bypass all of them. My plot was correct, so we returned to Dawson's "camp." The new trail was safe.

The tractor train had reached Crevasse Junction by now, so I brought Smitty back to supervise its passage through the region of crevasses.

While Young and Smitty made their plans for sending the first tractor through the "gulch," Speed and I took off for Little America.

Young had told me that some of his men were feeling "crevasse fever," so I sent Chaplain Peter Bol out to conduct services and do what he could to raise morale. He took along several bags of mail.

When he arrived, the first sled had been dragged to safety on the plateau. That in itself had raised morale a great deal. Then the men opened their mail from home, and morale was no longer a factor. One man got a sharply worded letter from the Internal Revenue Service ordering him to pay his taxes within five days. Another got a "Dear John" letter from his girl friend. Both letters, so completely unexpected under the circumstances, shifted the men's minds from the seriousness of the business at hand.

Slowly and carefully, each tractor and sled was taken across the seven-and-a-half-mile area. At first a twelve-hour interval passed between loads to allow the ice to settle. When no fissures opened, the interval was reduced to six hours. Soon ten of the twelve sleds were on the plateau.

Driver Ben Melton had dragged the tenth sled and was

returning in his empty tractor when he realized a "cat-skinner's nightmare." His heavy machine skidded to one side, and he felt the rear end sink. Instinctively he knew he had cracked a snow bridge. All logic cried out for him to abandon his vehicle immediately, but he applied more power and drove it to safety.

Young and Smitty had trailed Melton in the weasel and had witnessed his near-escape. The snow bridge was blasted away, and Smitty was lowered into the crevasse to investigate.

From some sixty feet below the surface, he relayed instructions to the men above.

"Have a man walk from the edge of the crevasse in the direction of the camp with trail markers. . . . There—tell him to plant a marker there! . . . Now tell him to walk some more. . . . Stop! Mark that spot! . . . Now tell him to walk to his right. . . . There! Plant another marker!"

When Smitty emerged from the hole he said that the path marked by trail flags would be safe for the remaining two loads.

"How the hell could you see a man through thirty feet of ice?" Young demanded.

"Oh, you can see all right. Remember, down there I'm in the dark, but a man on the surface is silhouetted against the sky. His image gets weaker or stronger, depending on the thickness of the snow."

"Well, how thick is the bridge you told him to mark?" Young asked.

"I'd estimate it is at least thirty feet thick. We are taking a risk, of course, but I'd rather try driving across that natural bridge than take time to blast the lid and fill the crevasse. We don't have too much time to waste."

Melton volunteered to follow Smitty's recommended trail with the next sled. Young asked if he wanted to use reins to steer the tractor over the dangerous path, but he spurned the idea. Smitty climbed onto the tractor's cat-walk and gave precise instructions as Melton navigated across to safety.

In one more pass the last sled was pulled to the plateau. The train formed up once more and began the long uphill trek to the site of Byrd Station.

In planning the tractor swing we realized that, once the vehicles attained the plateau, they would require bulk delivery of fuel by aircraft. To transport enough fuel for a six-tractor train by small R4D Navy planes would have been time-consuming and extremely expensive beyond the two-hundred-fifty-mile point. We had therefore arranged for the Air Force planes that were making the Pole drops from McMurdo to parachute fuel loads along the trail to Byrd Station.

By radio I could tell the air squadron commander where Dawson's advance party would be at a given date, so that he could deposit several tons of fuel in drums. Dawson's crew would recover the drops and cache the fuel alongside the trail for pick-up by Young's train. In the event of blizzards, the caches would be marked with trail flags. By December 11, Skip was ready to receive the first drop.

I radioed his position to Lieutenant Colonel Ellen, the air squadron commander, and asked for a ten-ton drop. Skip was at mile 480 from Little America, so that Ellen's round trip from McMurdo Sound would be in excess of 1,600 miles. While each drop would be accomplished in minutes, the whole flight would require nearly twelve hours. To this day I shudder at the cost of Diesel fuel delivered in such a manner; but it was still the cheapest way.

I advised Ellen that time was of the essence, and that Dawson would keep moving until he learned the planes were on their way. The closer he could place the drop pallets to the trail, the better. I said, "If you can't stack it neatly we will accept as delivered."

When I learned the Globemaster was en route to make the drop the afternoon of December 11 I began monitoring the voice radio circuit. Skip's voice told me the plane was in his vicinity.

"Air Force 207, this is trail party. We have you in sight bearing 090 grid, approximately ten miles. Do you see me?"

Ellen's voice replied: "Trail party, this is Air Force 207. Have you in sight dead ahead. Stand by for drop."

From Dawson: "Roger. Drop zone south of trail is marked by orange strip."

Ellen made a pass, and parachutes streamed from the belly of his large plane. On the ends of the shrouds were neatly bundled drums of fuel. The drop was made from low altitude, and it did not take long for the cargo to reach the snow.

Minutes passed. Then Ellen's voice came over the air: "There it goes, over to the south. When you reach the parachute this time, cut the lines. To hell with saving the chute!"

Again the air waves were silent. Finally Skip's voice: "All drums recovered. Thank you very much."

Ellen turned his plane back toward McMurdo Sound. His next drop would be at mile 563.

In his situation report that evening Skip said nothing about chasing the parachute seven miles on foot and by weasel! Wind had caught the huge chute and dragged the pallet of fuel drums as if it were weightless.

Meanwhile, Vic Young's tractor train was rumbling along in good shape until a push rod was broken on one of the engines. I received a request for a spare part but could not launch an airplane because of bad weather.

The train had been sitting idle for two days, and Young's disgust showed in his situation report: "Anchored as before. Need push rod."

Every attempt to deliver the part had failed. When weather was clear for take-off from Little America the tractor train was socked in. When weather cleared there, Little America was in the midst of a blizzard. Young was eager to get under way, but I rationalized that the spare part was not so urgently needed that it would warrant risking the loss of an airplane. I wished he had the disposition to apply *patience*, the hall-mark of Antarctic success.

Vic's report December 14 amazed me: "Made push rod. Train under way. Part not imperative now."

Just how Young had managed to fix the broken push rod more than two hundred miles out on the ice, I could not guess. Long ago, however, I ceased being surprised at the ingenuity of Navy Seabees. They cannot be held down. The "how" was not nearly so important as the fact that Young's party was under way.

Finally the weather improved, and I had begun sending fuel to the two-hundred-fifty-mile point by the R4D's when I learned how the tractor part had been repaired.

"Cal Larsen fixed it," Young said.

Now there was a surprise. Cal Larsen was a photographer, the only non-Seabee on the train!

"Where I come from," Larsen explained, "we never let a tractor sit idle. When Montana wheat is ready to be harvested it doesn't wait for tractors to be repaired.

"I saw a steel rod the cook used to keep pots from sliding off the stove. The stem was almost exactly the same diameter as the push rod. We dug the broken part out of the snow, snipped off the good end, and fused it with the pot holder. It worked fine."

Equipment problems were not peculiar to the tractor crews. The aircraft suffered as well. Once while flying gasoline to the two-hundred-fifty-mile cache Speed got stranded. All along I had wondered why it had taken us so long to get airborne when we landed on the trail. Speed had presumed his plane was overloaded. We always flew in that condition. We had to, and I didn't question his judgment. But at the trail fuel cache he realized what caused his sluggish take offs. The neoprene coating on his airplane's skis had broken and the metal of the skis was exposed to the ice. Rarely can a more solid physical marriage be achieved than between ice and metal.

Speed dumped his load of fuel into the storage tanks and tried to take off for the return flight to Little America. His plane would not budge. He spent several hours trying to shake the craft free but was unsuccessful. Finally he radioed that he would have to remain on the trail until another plane could fly JATO bottles to him.

By the time the JATO arrived Speed had used so much

fuel that he barely made it back to Little America. The skis on his plane were replaced, and he never had trouble taking off again.

Skip's advance party arrived at Byrd Station site December 16, one month and ten days after leaving Little America. Byrd Station was not different from all the miles of snow Dawson had already seen. In every direction there was nothing to break the monotony of the white landscape. On arrival, Tex Gardiner and Big Ed Edwards bulldozed a huge snow mound on the spot Mogensen computed to be Latitude 80° South, Longitude 120° West.

Tex voiced the feelings of the trail party when he produced an empty whiskey bottle, scrawled a note, and climbed the snow mound to plant his crude capsule. Inside the bottle was a message that proclaimed:

"Know ye, one and all. This land, as far as the eye can see, is hereby claimed in the name of the great state of Texas.

"Tex Gardiner, Seabee, United States Navy
"Sometimes called the Dirty Bearded Texan"

Dawson's report that his goal had been attained brought an avalanche of congratulatory messages from persons high in government, science, and military circles. My congratulations to him were minimized by the prominence of incoming praise. None, however, could have been more heartfelt.

But the job was not yet complete.

The ice airstrip at McMurdo Sound had become almost untenable as the "summer" season wore on. Great melt-water holes formed wherever oil had been spilled on the runway and deep gouges had been made in the ice by planes landing. Tidal action threatened to destroy the strip at any moment.

Colonel Ellen realized the seriousness of our fuel needs and kept enough planes at McMurdo to finish supporting the tractor operations before evacuating his big planes to New Zealand. He knew that if all the tractors in Young's train could not be provided with fuel when they arrived at Byrd Station, some would have to remain idle there. This of course would result in a smaller train to deliver the remaining cargo to complete Byrd Station.

As soon as Dawson reached the base site Ellen launched his planes. They dropped more than thirty tons of fuel directly on 80° South, 120° West, then hastened back to McMurdo Sound to refuel for the flight to New Zealand.

With the base site a reality and with Young's tractor train making good speed there with cargo to begin building the camp I felt elated when Admiral Dufek's message arrived to take the wind out of my sails:

"For Commander Frazier. Have you checked position of Byrd Base by celestial fix? If operating conditions permit, it is desired to have this base at (exactly) 80° South, 120° West. Please advise."

That message put me at a complete loss. It was the only time I have ever been provoked at Admiral Dufek. He had given me a mission and, I assumed, trusted my judgment. I had reported the mission accomplished, so what more did he want?

I radioed: "Position checked by sun lines and is definitely within one mile accuracy, and possibly one-half mile. Further sights will reduce error to 100 feet. This is the best we can hope for. I have used every means available, short of a rubber straight edge."

I am still surprised the Admiral did not discipline me for my impertinence. One just doesn't talk that way to an admiral. He must have understood how I felt. Months later I learned what had prompted his challenging message. Rumor had spread that the trail party was rushing pellmell to the base site without taking time for accurate navigation. On hearing this the scientists had gone to him for confirmation. He was merely telling me to be precise, and I had misinterpreted his meaning.

On December 19 Vic Young reported the tractor train at mile 404. The trail was still uphill, but with the increased altitude the snow crust was harder and the loads could be pulled faster. That was the day Skip turned around to go back to Little America. Any day now, I could expect to hear that the two parties had met on the trail. I was fully prepared to authorize both leaders to "splice the main brace" with medicinal alcohol in celebration of their meeting.

They met December 22. Barely taking time for Mogensen to brief Chief Surveyor George Moss on the location of the cairn his party had marked, Dawson headed for Little America, and Young continued on for Byrd Station. Neither had allowed the drivers to switch off the tractors' engines.

Young arrived at Byrd Station site December 23 with cargo to build four huts. Within nine hours the first building was completed. Men who were not busy unloading sleds or assembling the first building were put to work recovering the fuel that had been airdropped.

I could feel well pleased now. The mission, for all

practical purposes, was completed. There was some repair work for Dawson's party at Crevasse Junction, and a second tractor swing was required before all cargo was delivered; but we knew it could be done without a great deal of worry from here on in.

I never got to see Byrd Station. I had flown over the area before the base was built; but now the planes that were flying food, scientific equipment, and construction men out to complete the base were already overloaded, so I declined Speed's offer to see what the camp looked like. Besides, I reasoned, if I could say I had not seen the base there would be less trouble preventing other "tourists" from bumming rides on the heavily laden airplanes.

I was content to rest on my laurels and bask in the compliments that had been paid us for the way the trail job was done and the cargo delivered. From now to the end of Deep Freeze II, I thought, there'll be no more worry from me. I will just bide my time until the operation is over and I can be with my family once more.

But Admiral Dufek had other ideas. He radioed that I was to turn the trail responsibility over to somebody else and take over as task unit commander in charge of getting cargo unloaded from the ships arriving at Little America.

I do not deny that I was pleased to get command of three ships—an icebreaker and two cargo vessels; but in the weeks to come I was to learn that some of the headaches of trail blazing were minor, compared to the circumstances that would arise before the ships were unloaded.

18 ————————————————————

I HAD been mildly disappointed at not being able to see Byrd Station after the many hours and difficult decisions the project had cost; but I felt duly compensated when Admiral Dufek showed such confidence in me that he appointed me Task Unit Commander of the three ships arriving at Little America. My mind flashed back to Deep Freeze I when we faced so many obstacles in getting the ships unloaded, so I knew my next job would not be a push-over.

Tex Gardiner's left-handed compliment on the eve of the trail party's departure came back to mind, too: "We knew you from last year, and at times you were a pretty rough bas—you've been a pretty tough customer." Admiral Dufek undoubtedly thought along the same lines: When there's a rough job to do, pick a rough bastard to do it.

Over the past few months, while the trail was being blazed to Byrd Station, Pemmican Jack Bursey and I had skied from Little America to the water's edge in Kainan Bay once a week to inspect the bay ice. There was a beautiful natural ramp sloping down from the ice shelf to the bay ice. The usual tidal crack at the top of the ramp had been filled; but there was another three-foot crack in the bay ice about a mile from the edge of the barrier which we presumed could be bridged. The bay ice was nine feet thick and unloading appeared to pose no problem once the crack was spanned.

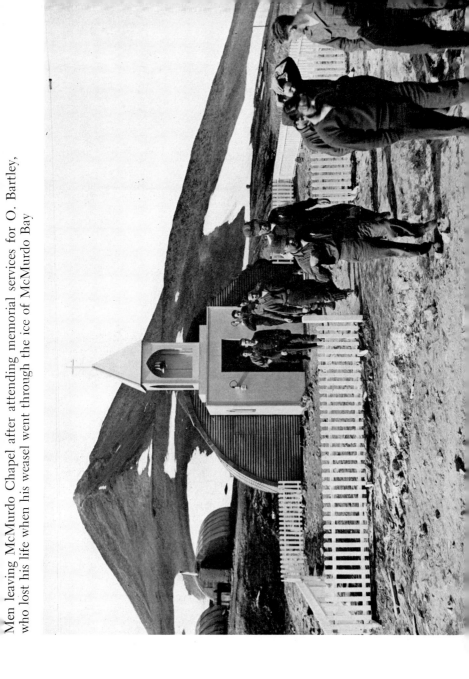

Men leaving McMurdo Chapel after attending memorial services for O. Bartley, who lost his life when his weasel went through the ice of McMurdo Bay

Preparations are made to blast a safe mooring site along the loose ice of the Ross Shelf in Kainan Bay.

The USNS *Pvt. Joseph F. Merrell* races against time to unload crucial supplies on to the shelf at Kainan Bay.

Personnel evacuating to the USS *Atka* for the long voyage home.

A few penguins walked around on the bay ice, and a herd of seals lay dormant near the large tide crack out in the bay. I flagged a trail from the end of the ramp out to the ice edge, placing four flags where the bridge would be installed to span the crack.

Unloading this year would be a snap! With good, solid bay ice and a natural ramp to the barrier we would snake the twelve thousand tons of cargo from shipside to the base in something like fourteen working days. *I thought.*

Open water reached north from the bay ice, and the faint outline of the ice pack could be detected on the horizon. The high ice cliffs surrounding Kainan Bay reflected the midday sun as Jack and I surveyed the situation. The temperature was fifteen below zero, but we were sweating as we completed our last reconnaissance on December 23. I took off my shirt and wrapped it around my waist as we headed back for Little America. There was no wind, the sky was cloudless, and the sun felt good on my damp body. Without sunglasses the glare was blinding, and I put them back on. I felt like a business executive enjoying a Turkish bath after putting over an important deal. The trail was blazed to Byrd Station, the first tractor train was completed, and I had myself a three-ship command. Who could ask for more?

When we returned to Little America a message was waiting: Admiral Dufek directed the *Atka, Merrell,* and *Greenville Victory* to leave McMurdo Sound at 8 A.M. December 27 and proceed to Little America. On arrival, each commanding officer would report to me for instructions.

I sent a message to Commander Charlie Bulfinch of the *Atka* the same day, requesting a conference on arrival.

He was to order his helicopter to pick up the other ship commanders, the supply officers and Seabees who would be responsible for getting the cargo ashore at Little America. I planned to move aboard the *Atka*.

Captain Bulfinch replied that he would arrive early in the morning of December 28. The conference was set for 8 A.M. that day.

The weather was beautiful when *Atka* and the cargo ships arrived. *Atka*'s helicopter transported me to the ship. Lieutenant Commander Bill Harris, the executive officer, met me on the flight deck and took me to join the Captain at breakfast in his cabin.

Charlie turned the task unit over to me and told me everyone was ready in the wardroom for the conference. I asked him to begin breaking out a mooring site while the meeting was in session so that as soon as it ended we could commence unloading. He went to the bridge, and I stepped down the ladder to the wardroom.

It was quite an honor to be designated task unit commander of three ships. Everyone was calling me "Commodore." I had a good thing here if I didn't foul it up.

"Gentlemen, my name is Frazier. I have been placed in command of this task unit to unload cargo at Little America. I know most of you from last year and know what a good job you can do. However, let us review our mission.

"The only objective is to get the cargo from the ships to the base. We have two miles of bay ice and three miles of shelf ice to transit. There is one tide crack about a mile this side of the base of the ramp which has to be bridged. We will use bridging material that is in number three hold of the *Greenville Victory*. Another tide crack at the top of

[210]

the ramp has been filled. There are three crevasses in the valley one mile from Little America. They have been checked and filled.

"The *Atka* is now breaking out a mooring for the *Merrell* and *Greenville Victory*. *Greenville Victory* will moor first and unload the bridging material for the tide crack. When the crack is bridged, general off-loading will commence and will continue around the clock.

"Lieutenant Fred Whipple of the *Atka* is designated beachmaster. He is responsible for getting cargo over the sides of the ships to the sleds.

"Chief Warrant Officer George Purinton is in charge of the tractors, and he will report to me daily the number of tractors available for unloading and the number of tractors under maintenance.

"Ice safety is paramount. The trail will be checked three times a day. All vehicles will stay on the marked trail. Personnel leaving the ships and the base will be checked out and in so we know where everybody is.

"If the ice begins to break up it is the duty of the first person who sees it to notify Whipple or me and to discontinue unloading. If possible, the tractors and sleds will be returned to Little America. But if the ice cracks at a point between the tractors and the base, each cargo ship will have slings ready for lifting the heavy equipment aboard on short notice.

"We will be in communication with Little America, each ship, the beachmaster, and a roving weasel on the trail. I don't think I need to remind you that the radio circuit is for business, not gossip."

There were a few questions, but in general everyone had been through this before.

"Remember one thing." I looked at Don Mehaffey. "The cargo is no good left on the ships. If there is any doubt as to whether it should be neatly stacked on the barrier or left on the ships, I'll settle it now. The cargo will be put on the ice shelf whether it is neatly stacked or not. This ice can go out at any time. We must have a rapid discharge."

Mehaffey groaned as he remembered the disorderly supply dump of the last year. I sympathized with him, but facts were facts. The cargo was no good on the ships or under the water; it must be on the shelf.

The conference ended, and I went to the bridge. Captain Bulfinch was doing a fine job breaking out a mooring. He would be through in about two hours, so I notified the *Greenville Victory* to stand ready to moor at noon.

Atka's crew dug holes in the bay ice and planted deadmen for the *Greenville Victory's* mooring lines.

Thirty minutes later, swells appeared from the open sea and cracked the bay ice. The deadmen floated to sea, and a morning's work was wasted.

I notified the *Greenville Victory* what had happened and asked the skipper to be ready to moor sometime in the late afternoon. Charlie Bulfinch began breaking out a new mooring area.

New deadmen were planted, but again the ice broke and went to sea. The whole day had been wasted. I decided to wait until the wind shifted and the swells calmed. All we were doing was wasting fuel. Charlie and I went below for coffee.

I sipped my coffee while Charlie put his *My Fair Lady* album on the phonograph. Soon the strains of "With a Little Bit of Luck" filled the cabin. The song was most appropriate. I could do nothing about the wind and sea, but with a little bit of luck we would get the cargo ashore.

Nearly half the ice in Kainan Bay went to sea December 29. More broke and drifted out December 30. Fred Whipple and I skied over the remaining ice trying to determine where it would be safe to unload when the wind shifted. In the afternoon we stood on the bridge and watched the ski tracks we had made in the morning float out to sea.

December 31 brought no change. The bay ice broke to within five hundred yards of the ramp, and hairline cracks showed in the ice that remained. Tide cracks near the edge of the remaining ice worked up and down as much as five inches. Reluctantly I radioed our dismal circumstances to the Admiral.

I did not realize that my problems at Little America were the least of the Admiral's worries. At Cape Adare the *Arneb* had been crushed in an ice jam, and her crew was waging a valiant effort to save the ship. In the Weddell Sea the *Wyandot* had been holed by the ice and was trapped, as was her escorting icebreaker. At McMurdo Sound the landing strip threatened to break up and float to sea before the Globemasters could return from New Zealand to complete their cargo drops at the Pole.

Dufek's Volunteers were catching hell from all directions.

The Admiral informed me that when we did moor he desired the *Greenville Victory* unloaded first so she could return to McMurdo. She had cargo for four stations, so it was imperative that she get under way as soon as possible. But I had to get the sleds off the *Merrell* before I could get to the *Greenville Victory*.

I stood on *Atka*'s bridge and watched the ice go to sea. The high ice shelf surrounding the open water of the bay looked ugly. To unload cargo over a shelf a hundred feet high was impossible. The low area of ice to the south was heavily crevassed. It was the same section we had surveyed last year when we needed so urgently to unload a search plane from the *Eastwind*.

Unless some bay ice remained after the wind and swells died, there would not be any unloading at Little America. That meant the cargo would have to be returned to McMurdo Sound and air-dropped to Little America and Byrd Station if there was going to be any food and fuel for the men during the coming winter.

Meantime, *Nespelen* arrived from McMurdo Sound with 100,000 gallons of aviation gasoline which she was supposed to pump ashore at Little America. Since the discharge of fuel did not require heavy tractors and sleds to come alongside the ship, I ordered the *Atka* to shave the edge off the lower section of the ice shelf in the southeast corner of Kainan Bay. Men on skis could safely walk across the crevassed ice to handle *Nespelen*'s fuel lines, and she could begin discharging fuel while we waited for the swells to stop so that the cargo ships could be brought to safe moorings.

An icebreaker had never been pitted against the ice barrier to my knowledge, so *Atka* was performing a "first," however dangerous it was. The danger lay in the fact that if she struck the ice from the wrong angle and caused it to cascade down on her decks the weight might heel her over.

I radioed Admiral Dufek that *Atka* had broken thirty-one million tons of ice from the barrier and thus surpassed

[214]

Glacier's record of Deep Freeze I. The feat was not nearly so significant to the over-all operation as it was to the morale of *Atka*'s valiant crew.

I took stock of the situation and was disheartened: I had been in command of my first task unit of ships for a week, and still did not have one ounce of cargo ashore. Recalling Admiral Dufek's remark when we were mooring the YOG's in Winter Quarters Bay I thought: Tahiti, here I come!

The cargo *had* to be off-loaded onto the shelf because there was not enough Globemasters to air-drop Pole Station, Byrd Station, and resupply cargo for Little America. Have patience, I told myself, and left the bridge to go below. The strains of "With a Little Bit of Luck" once more greeted me as I poured a cup of coffee. I set the cup down and returned to the bridge for another look.

The ice shelf was only about fifty feet high in the southeast corner of the bay. *Maybe* we could blast off fifteen or twenty feet of ice and *create* a low enough shelf for off-loading. Could the *Atka* break *into the crevasse* that ran out to the southeast from the site I had in mind? The crevasse's gaping interior was visible, covered with a three-foot snow bridge. I thought of the hours we had spent filling the part of the barrier that had gone to sea. The tracks of the trail ran into nothing over the edge of the high shelf.

I asked Charlie to see what the *Atka* could do with the shelf. He charged the edge of the crevasse and tons of ice crumbled onto the forecastle. He withdrew and charged again. The forecastle was a mass of white, and other large pieces of ice the size of houses bobbed up from the depths of the water.

Charlie had found the weak point. He withdrew from

the cavern, and the crew began throwing blocks of ice over the starboard side of the bow.

When the forecastle was clear Charlie charged the shelf again. Ice crumbled down again, and more large chunks surfaced menacingly ahead.

We were now a full ship's length into the crevasse.

Charlie broke to the right and left, peeling off more ice. The ship's crew was tireless. After every three lunges the forecastle had to be cleared. The railings and breakwater lay smashed flat on deck, but some damage had to be expected. We had a job to do.

By now we had penetrated so far into the crevasse that I could just see over the edge of the ice shelf from the *Atka*'s bridge. It was too high to discharge cargo, so we had to find some way of lowering the shelf.

I called George Purinton on the radio. "George, I need a D-8 tractor at the barrier edge as soon as possible."

Then I turned to Charlie Bulfinch. "Charlie, I would like to use your mooring wire to cut the snow off the ice shelf. There is a tractor on the way. Will you lay out wire from your port side? Pass the bitter end to the tractor. As the wire is dragged by the tractor I hope to shave the shelf down to size."

I knew I was gambling with human lives and precious equipment, and the thought frightened me. The risk was necessary, however, if the bases were to be supplied.

George sent the tractor immediately. The long wire was made fast, and it cut into the crusty snow. Loosened snow tumbled down on the whole port side of the *Atka*, but the maneuver was successful. The barrier was now low enough to work cargo over.

"Moor the *Merrell*," I ordered, guarding my voice

against betrayal of emotion. David had challenged Goliath and won.

"With a Little Bit of Luck" was still playing when I poured myself a hot cup of coffee and sat down. Today I could file my first progress report.

Before we could get to the items in the *Merrell's* hold we had to unload two crated Otter airplanes that blocked her cargo hatches. They were light but bulky and were sitting at a forty-five-degree angle, one end on the ship and one end on the ice shelf when I came topside. There appeared to be a stalemate, because that was as high as the *Merrell's* booms could hoist the bulky crates.

But George Purinton saved the day. He passed wires around the crates and a D-8 tractor dragged them up on the shelf. The planes were damaged slightly, but maintenance crews could repair them later. The way they were unloaded, I was amazed that they were not damaged more.

Two landing boats still had to be snaked onto the barrier before cargo could be discharged. They were veterans of World War II invasions and were sturdy enough to stand the strain without being bashed in.

Unloading from the *Merrell* went smoothly. The wind shifted from the southeast, but now the high shelf sheltered the ship so that she rode snugly against the face of the barrier. Cargo hooks dipped into the holds and raised parcels of supplies into the air, where another line from a boom-rigged tractor pulled them to a sled some twenty feet from the edge of the ice.

A slight swell began undercutting the ice shelf where *Merrell* was moored. On January 4 I ordered the ship to unmoor lest she become holed by the overhanging ledge. Further, there was danger of ten feet of ice crashing down on the thin-skinned ship. If that happened, the tractors, sleds, and men might be hurled into the water.

Atka towed *Merrell* away from the shelf face, and she steamed out of the bay while I pondered our problem.

I had seen explosives used on ice many times to no avail. Somehow we had to break off the overhanging ten feet of ice for safety.

I explained my problem to Herb Whitney and asked whether he thought shaped charges placed in line about ten feet from the edge would cut the ice.

"I don't know," he said, "but let's give it a try."

It seems to me that Boom Boom Wedemeyer's love for blasting, manifested in the latrine incident, is common to all Seabees, and they relish the sound of a loud explosion.

There was no shortage of explosives now that the ships had arrived, so I told Herb to give the venture a try. He supervised the placement of ten shaped charges some twenty feet apart and ten feet back from the edge of the ice shelf. From the bridge of the *Atka*, about five hundred feet off the barrier, I watched.

Herb pointed to the charges and waved a red flag. I waved back, indicating that all was ready for the experiment.

Boom!

From across the bay the high cliffs of ice echoed the blast.

BOOM! Boom! *Boom!* I heard from three sides of the bay.

Ice dropped into the sea, leaving a smooth, neatly cut face. Ten more charges farther along finished the job.

We used the same procedure each time water undercut the barrier where a ship was unloading. Once the *Atka*'s nose was a bit too close to the blast scene, and a huge section of the barrier the size of an iceberg falling into the sea surfaced so close that the little icebreaker rolled sixty degrees. A few feet closer and she would have been destroyed.

We docked the *Greenville Victory*. One heavy D-8 tractor was loaded on deck and the ship's cargo booms could not reach the distance to the ice shelf with so heavy a weight. Yet, we could not unload the number three hold until the tractor was lifted ashore.

"How long is that Bailey bridge you've got?" I asked George Purinton.

"We have three fifteen-foot sections," he answered.

"The distance from the side of the ship to the top of the shelf is about forty feet. The angle is about fifty degrees. Can the bridge support thirty-seven tons?"

"No, sir. It has to be supported in the middle."

I turned to Smith, the chief boatswain's mate in charge of unloading.

"If we assemble the bridge and put it into place, then put the tractor on the end supported by the ship, can you take the slings off the tractor and attach them to the middle of the bridge?"

"Sure, Commander," the chief replied, "but it will mean somebody's got to *drive* the tractor up the bridge!"

If the ship rolled as much as five degrees while the tractor was so delicately balanced, we would lose one vehicle and one driver. I dreaded asking for a volunteer driver, but Chief Petty Officer Taylor of the Seabees must have read my thoughts. He volunteered by climbing into the driver's seat and giving me a wave.

I instructed George Purinton to anchor the shore side of the bridge with two tractors. A third would pull the D-8 monster up the slippery surface of the aluminum bridge.

It took nine hours to rig the bridge and get it placed just right. The span barely reached the edge of the barrier, and we held our breath and crossed our fingers when the D-8 was placed on the edge of it. The slings were removed and attached to the center of the bridge. All was in readiness.

George Purinton raised his arm and moved it in a rotary motion. The ship's winch took a strain on the bridge, the pulling tractor on the ice took a strain on its line, and Chief Taylor revved up his engine and engaged the gears.

Slowly the tractor was drawn up the bridge to the edge of the shelf. Had not the engines been running we could have heard a pin drop on deck.

Inch by inch the monster approached the barrier. Finally its wide tracks brushed against the snow and began biting into the surface. The near edge of the shelf sent snow cascading into the sea. Within a few feet the tracks took hold, and the tractor helped itself the remainder of the way to safety. The wire was released, and we now had another machine to haul sleds.

With a little bit of luck? Already we had had more than our share, I thought. My situation report asked the Admiral to commend Purinton, Taylor, and Smith.

Nespelen had been standing by since January 5 to begin discharging aviation gasoline. The Marines had nearly completed laying out three miles of hose from the tank at Little America to the ship. *Greenville Victory*'s unloading was completed January 8, so I brought the *Nespelen* in to discharge her fuel. Larry Sup, her skipper, nosed the little tanker into the barrier and took aboard the end of the pipeline. Soon he was discharging gasoline at his maximum rate.

The face of the ice shelf again needed cutting. I had undocked the *Greenville Victory* and would blast off the overhang before docking *Merrell,* but I thought the overhang would hold until *Nespelen* finished pumping gasoline ashore.

She was riding about a hundred feet off the face of the shelf with her bow pointed toward it and her propellers turning over. Suddenly the whole face of the barrier on her port side crumbled and crashed into the sea. *Nespelen* rolled and bobbed like a cork. Her crew quickly released the ship's fuel lines, and the ship backed clear of the ice. No damage was done, but it had been a near miss.

Captain Sup called me by radio to report what had happened. He didn't have to explain. I had seen it. "Sorry, Larry. I should have had that face blasted before you moored, but I thought it would hold. Remoor in the same spot. There is nothing left to break off for the next few days."

Sup nosed his craft back into position and began discharging again. He finished pumping January 9 and recovered his fuel hose. The tanks at Little America were full, so I ordered *Nespelen* to return to McMurdo Sound.

Dawson's trail party had remained in the crevasse region on the trail until the empty tractors returned from Byrd Station. The train arrived at Little America January 5, and Dawson's group returned a day later. It was good to have his advice on our ice problems at the barrier's edge and to have the spare tractors available to pull cargo away from the ships. In case we had to shift moorings to the south edge of Kainan Bay I wanted Dawson to have a safe trail blazed and filled through the crevasses to Little America.

Merrell's unloading was proceeding satisfactorily. Every three days we would tow her out, blast off the face of the shelf and remoor. The operation was becoming routine. Then a storm broke the monotony.

The wind and sea now came from the northwest, and the *Merrell* bobbed up and down beside the face of the shelf. With so much of her cargo removed, she rode light and high in the water. A swell lifted her and set her down on an ice foot, punching a hole in her side below the waterline.

The crew started the emergency pumps and rigged mattresses over the hole as *Atka* pulled her away from the shelf to safety. The storm continued.

Within a few hours giant waves pounded the unloading site and the southern reaches of Kainan Bay. Large sections of the shelf broke off and floated to sea as tabular icebergs.

The walls of the crevasse in the valley near Little America were surging up and down as much as three inches, even though the crevasse was two miles from the open sea. We feared that the whole section of ice shelf would break off and go to sea, leaving Little America perilously close to the water.

Merrell reported that her flooding was under control and she would be able to ride out the storm without further damage.

Swells pounding the ice shelf increased to seven feet. As more broke off we could see gaping holes which had been the interior of crevasses. The storm raged while we stood offshore and hoped for the best.

When the gale abated we had work to do. The ice shelf had been worn away as much as fifty feet in places. Ragged, sharp ice feet protruded beneath the water in the vicinity of the mooring site, and it was unsafe to bring a thin-hulled ship alongside. Unloading could not be done until this hurdle had been overcome.

I told Skip Dawson to blast a new mooring site, deep in the shelf. We had penetrated three hundred feet and would have to go three hundred feet more. I advised the Admiral of my intentions January 19.

Weather turned bad again. The entire western Ross Sea was free of ice, so that storms and swells which built up hundreds of miles to the northwest ran unimpeded in the direction of Kainan Bay.

Icebreakers were in short supply, I knew from reading the dispatches of the various task group commanders. The *Northwind* had a damaged propeller and was in New Zealand for repairs. *Glacier* was busy on Knox Coast. *Staten Island* in the Weddell Sea had a broken propeller blade.

I considered the Admiral's position. If things got any worse in the Weddell Sea, *Glacier* would have to be sent there in a hurry. Then *Atka* would be the only icebreaker available for the Ross Sea area.

I did not know when the weather would abate and allow us to finish unloading the *Merrell*. The bulk of the cargo was ashore, and what remained could be taken to Little America by air or by one of the crippled icebreakers.

I radioed the Admiral that *Merrell* might be indefinitely delayed by weather at Little America and suggested that my task unit return to McMurdo Sound. *Merrell's* cargo could be unloaded there, permitting her to return to America. Such a move, I explained, would free the tractors at Little America to make the second swing to Byrd Station. It would also save money in that the *Merrell* could be released much earlier.

The Admiral bought my idea. Charlie Bulfinch nosed the *Atka* into the barrier long enough to retrieve *Merrell's* mooring lines. Personnel and outgoing mail were taken aboard, and we sailed for McMurdo Sound early on January 21.

I hoped I would never have to account for *Merrell's* landing craft that sat high and dry on the ice shelf as we steamed away from Little America.

19

McMURDO SOUND was a mess when we arrived from Little America. An Antarctic heat wave, with noon temperatures reaching as high as forty degrees, threatened to wreck Operation Deep Freeze II.

From Admiral Dufek's situation reports to the Chief of Naval Operations I knew that the air strip was inoperable; but I did not realize how bad it was.

When I dissolved my task unit I walked across the ice to report to the Admiral. The ice edge was about three miles from Hut Point, and the trail used by the tractors as they dragged cargo ashore was a chain of potholes connected by masses of slush. Every spot where a piece of scrap lumber or other dunnage had been spilled was now a water hole.

The trail wound around unsafe areas and joined another which had been used to deliver air-drop cargo from the base to the airplanes. I walked out to the airstrip. That area was worst of all. My shoes were sodden from stepping into puddles as I inspected it.

In the middle of the strip seals stuck their heads up through holes, and penguins pranced around where ninety-ton aircraft had recently operated. I joined a group who identified themselves as the ice patrol. It was their duty to certify the trail safe or unsafe for the tractors dragging cargo from the ships.

We probed every pothole. At three feet we inevitably struck solid ice. By auger samplings, we learned that at the worst points along the trail the ice was still nine feet thick and thus safe for tractor operations. The ice patrol was extremely important to morale, because a few days earlier a party of six men had attempted to reach the frozen-in YOG's by weasel. As they left the trail some fifty yards behind, their vehicle broke through the ice and a man was drowned. Such an incident inevitably has a bad effect on drivers of heavy equipment.

The camp at McMurdo Sound looked as if it had been run through a wringer. Facilities had been overtaxed for months, and the place showed it. The camp had been designed to house ninety-three men, but since the beginning of air operations in October the population had averaged three hundred. The heat wave had melted several thousand tons of snow from the nearby hillsides. As the melt-water poured downhill and along the streets it created a muck in the lava ash that was so deep it overran our shoe tops. Electric cables strung along the earth were exposed to the tracks of snow vehicles and power disruptions were frequent.

Morale was low. Men who had spent the winter night at McMurdo Sound thought they would be able to go home as soon as the first ships arrived. But crisis after crisis had delayed the ships' sailing.

Even the news correspondents who remained were grumpy. They had been in the Antarctic long enough for the initial glamour to wear off, but each hoped for a flight to the Pole when air operations recommenced. They griped about the store hours, the shortage of water, and other minor inconveniences. As is always the case, those who griped loudest were the ones who did not venture far from the building in which they slept.

There was a good excuse for each inconvenience, but the groaners were not concerned with causes. For example, the tractors which hauled snow for the melters had to make longer and longer trips to the snow mine as the heat wave continued. The store operator was also a cargo handler. There was a line in the mess hall because there were too many people present.

Colder weather, the solution to all problems, was not predicted before February. Meantime, Dr. Andrew Assur of the Snow, Ice, and Permafrost Research Institute, was rushed from the United States to McMurdo Sound to begin "treatment" of the ice that comprised the airstrip.

Daily he worked, caring for each pothole much like a dentist treating a tooth. First he would clear all slush from the melt-water hole and fill it with crushed ice and fresh water. The next day he would again drain the hole, clean the edges, and refill it with crushed ice and fresh water. Slowly the holes began to fill from the bottom with strong ice.

While Dr. Assur worked with the airstrip, ship operations in other areas took a turn for the better. Captain Ketchum's task group was making progress erecting the base on the Knox Coast, Captain McDonald's group had finally penetrated the Weddell Sea ice to the Filchner Ice Shelf, and cargo was being unloaded. Cape Adare was a completed station; the tens of thousands of penguins had been herded, and camp construction had been completed after the ships left. The *Towle* was unloaded and had sailed for the States. *Nespelen* returned from Australia with a full cargo of gasoline which she pumped into the storage tanks at McMurdo, guaranteeing that for next year's operation the planes would have more than a million gallons of aviation gasoline.

By February 5, Dr. Assur reported that the airstrip problem was beaten. Within a week it would be safe for the heavy planes to land and take off. The Air Force was alerted in New Zealand, and the first plane landed February 10.

That was the Admiral's birthday. For two years running, he had scored an operational break-through on his birthday. Last year a plane which had been lost for seven days was found. This year the planes returned to complete the airdrop of cargo at Pole Station and Byrd Station. Men who, we had thought, might have to be evacuated because they did not have enough food and fuel to last the winter could now be cared for.

Day after day the big airplanes shuttled cargo to the Pole. Smaller plans had flown the scientists in before the supplies were all dropped. At first the larger craft flew only essentials; food and fuel. When that was delivered they dropped "nice-to-have" equipment. When the scientists at Pole Station began asking for Ping-pong balls and fresh eggs, we knew the mission was completed.

While the airplanes dropped cargo first to Pole Station and then to Byrd Station, ship unloading at McMurdo Sound continued. Soon there were two years' provisions at the air station, and the ships were nearly unloaded.

As the last drop missions were being flown, the *Northwind* returned from New Zealand and back-loaded the Little America cargo from the *Merrell* so that that ship could sail for home.

I knew Deep Freeze II was a success. Every base we had built on paper in Washington was now a reality on the ice. Every ship which had been damaged in the operation was being repaired and would be able to sail home.

Orange buildings erected by Seabees dotted the bleak Antarctic continent in seven spots, their circumference spanning nearly four million square miles. Scientists and their equipment had been delivered to Little America, Weddell Sea, Knox Coast, Byrd Station, and Pole Station, and the air station at McMurdo Sound was secure for the winter night. Relief crews had arrived aboard the seaplane tender *Curtiss*, which had as return passengers the men who had spent the previous winter night in Antarctica. They were bound for New Zealand and their first liberty in more than a year.

We commenced evacuating the staff to New Zealand by air. I was directed to take the first half with me and to set up shop there for Admiral Dufek, who would arrive two days later.

I walked up the ramp and into the body of the Globemaster, gave my name to the crew chief who was checking passengers aboard, and fastened my safety belt. As soon as we were airborne I stretched out on top of a generator unit and went to sleep. It was going to be a long trip, and I intended to sleep for twelve hours. Mount Erebus did not hold any fascination for me now.

When I awoke, we were approaching McMurdo Sound —not New Zealand. The plane had developed engine trouble about halfway and had returned to the ice runway. After repairs were made we took off again, arriving in New Zealand at 3 A.M.

The bus taking us to our hotel bumped down Papanui Road. There was little traffic at this hour, and the town seemed deserted; but New Zealand was a beautiful sight under any circumstances.

[229]

As far as I was concerned, Deep Freeze II was over. Tomorrow I could start planning Deep Freeze III. The Admiral had told me that I was to be Assistant Chief of Staff for Plans and Operations for next year's operations. I was proud of my promotion, but even more pleased that he trusted my judgment.

Sleep took over, and I didn't wake until the maid brought in the morning tea. It was seven A.M. a day later. I had slept the clock around, with four hours to spare.

OPERATION DEEP FREEZE III

20 _____

PLANNING for Operation Deep Freeze III required less effort than the preceding operations. The task was simply to relieve the scientists and support crews who had wintered over, and reprovision the bases for the crews who would man the bases until the end of the International Geophysical Year. No further construction was required.

Of course there had to be ships to carry men and cargo, icebreakers to escort the cargo ships, and airplanes to fly drop missions as well as ski-planes to deliver men and non-droppable cargo.

We pored over the ship and airplane schedules, tonnages and delivery dates, and substituted better ways of doing the job based on experience in two years of operations.

Periodically during the summer we received reports from the Antarctic that the year of science was in full progress and that a new world's low temperature of 102.1 degrees below zero had been recorded at the South Pole.

Since Admiral Richard E. Byrd's death, Admiral Dufek had held two Antarctic responsibilities. As Commander of Task Force 43 and Commander, Naval Support Forces Antarctica, he was charged with supporting American scientists who were taking part in the Geophysical Year. As officer-in-charge, U.S. Antarctic Projects, the job he inherited from Admiral Byrd, he was responsible to the Government for various legislative and political projects concerning Antarctica.

Just before the ships and airplanes were to depart for the Antarctic in the fall of 1957, Admiral Dufek and I were flying to a conference with the Commander in Chief, Atlantic Fleet.

"Paul," he said, "I want you to be my Chief of Staff for Antarctic Projects."

"Yes, sir."

Those words put me into an office and behind a desk within a stone's throw of the White House and made me responsible for the Antarctic Projects office during the Admiral's absence.

I was disappointed at not being able to participate in Deep Freeze III as Operations Officer, but the new title had many assets. I could bring my family from Missouri to Washington and begin acting like a father again; I would not have to endure privations on the ice; and I could hope to render good service to Admiral Dufek, who had shown me so much confidence over the years.

Again I had a good thing if I didn't foul it up.

Once more I thought back to Tex Gardiner's remark at the impromptu beer party at Little America: "We knew you from last year, and at times you were a pretty rough bas—you've been a pretty tough customer." I wondered why the Admiral had chosen a "rough bastard" for so delicate a job, but was extremely pleased that he had.

It was most unusual to watch Deep Freeze III unfold from the vantage point of a mahogany desk in Washington. Each time I saw a report that a ship or a group of ships had performed its mission on schedule I was pleased; for, much as I yearned to be there, I took pride in telling myself that I had helped write the operation plan.

I was actually envious when I read that the unloading operation at Little America had been completed in six days. Somebody had had more than "a little bit of luck," I reasoned, or perhaps Nature was giving us a break after giving us hell for two years in a row.

Being on shore duty, I have had to make public speeches on various occasions about my Antarctic experiences. For one who has given so many years to Polar work, I suppose I should have developed some profound opinions on what Antarctica is worth, how it can be tamed, and how America should go about exploiting the ice-locked continent.

I have had my share of unusual experiences there and have heard many ideas advanced, some of them quite sound and some which impressed me as being hairbrained. Ideas on the Antarctic have run a great range. Admiral Byrd offered one of the most plausible when he proposed that the continent be used as a natural deep freeze to store food during years of plenty for years of want. Others have recommended mining coal, oil, and precious gems which may or may not exist. Still others would use the Antarctic as a base of military operations; their ideas range from an A-bomb testing ground to ice-locked bullpens for submarine operations.

The most important use of the Antarctic is as a scientific platform. Geophysics still has many secrets that the Antarctic area can help discover.

But I have always managed to keep a little man's perspective about the Antarctic. I feel extremely proud that I have been permitted to take part in Operation Deep Freeze, especially as one of Dufek's Volunteers supporting our scientists in their quest for knowledge.

I think the International Geophysical Year is a fine idea, and I am confident that, when the figures are tabulated and the findings interpreted, the world will be much better off as a result of the studies that have been made in the Antarctic.

I would like very much to see the average American become better educated about the Antarctic. On altogether too many occasions I have been asked such questions as:

How cold is it *up* there?

How big are the *polar bears* in the Antarctic?

Who *owns* Antarctica?

Are the *natives* friendly?

I am also asked *why* man goes to the Antarctic in the first place and, "If he has been there once, *why in the world* would he ever go back?"

To this question I can only answer for myself, because each man's reasons are his own. I have known men to turn explorer for personal recognition, for escape, for adventure. One man even went "because there are no women there."

I went first because I received a set of orders to duty on the staff of Task Force 39. I went back for seconds to see more of what I had missed seeing the first time. My third tour of duty there intrigued me more. There is something about putting your foot where no one else has ever stepped on before that fascinates me.

I do not have the power to see the Antarctic through the eyes of a poet. I know it is beautiful, and I also know it is cruel.

My approach is mundane. Antarctica is a place just like any other place, but it offers a challenge that other places don't.

Dufek's Volunteers at McMurdo Sound erected a sign just before the main entrance to camp. It read: "There is no place any place like this place so this must be the place."

I agree with them.

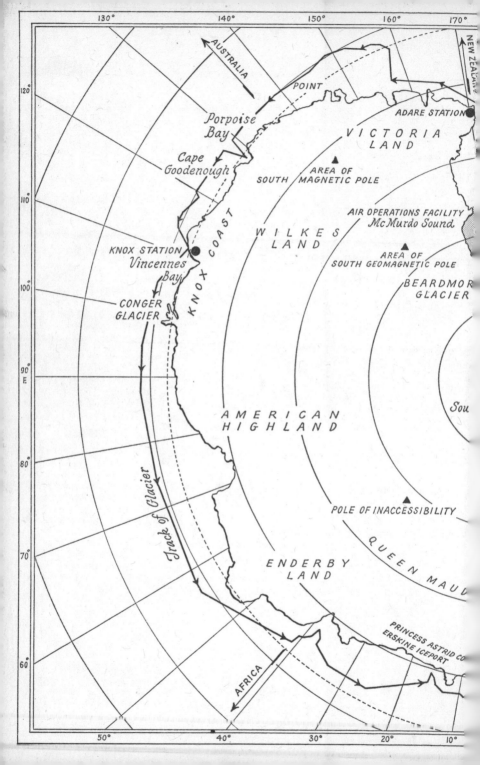